ALICE MEYERS

Confidence Unlocked

A Comprehensive Guide to Build Self-Assurance in the Workplace, Overcome Self-Doubt, and Build Habits for Success

Copyright © 2025 by Alice Meyers

All rights reserved. No part of this publication may be reproduced, stored or transmitted in any form or by any means, electronic, mechanical, photocopying, recording, scanning, or otherwise without written permission from the publisher. It is illegal to copy this book, post it to a website, or distribute it by any other means without permission.

Alice Meyers has no responsibility for the persistence or accuracy of URLs for external or third-party Internet Websites referred to in this publication and does not guarantee that any content on such Websites is, or will remain, accurate or appropriate.

First edition

This book was professionally typeset on Reedsy.
Find out more at reedsy.com

Contents

Introduction	v
Chapter 1: Building the Foundation of Confidence	1
Exploring the Psychological Aspects of Confidence	2
The Psychology of Resilience	6
Assessing Personal Strengths and Weaknesses	7
Setting Realistic and Achievable Goals	13
Developing a Positive Self-Image	18
Chapter 2: Overcoming Impostor Syndrome	25
What Are the Signs of Impostor Syndrome?	26
Analyzing the Root Causes	30
Breaking the Cycle of Self-Doubt	35
Building Self-Validation Practices	41
Chapter 3: Enhancing Communication Skills	48
Practicing Active Listening	49
Articulating Thoughts Clearly and Confidently	53
Understanding Non-Verbal Cues	56
Adapting Communication Styles	59
Chapter 4: Thriving Under Pressure	63
Managing Time Effectively	64
Utilizing Stress-Reduction Techniques	67
Prioritizing Tasks Under Pressure	71
Learning from Failure	74
Chapter 5: Navigating Discrimination and Bias	78
Recognizing Unconscious Biases	79
Communicating Assertively Against Discrimination	82

Building Allyship and Support Systems	85
Documenting and Reporting Incidents	89
Chapter 6: Boosting Self-Esteem	94
Practicing Self-Compassion	95
Reinforcing Positive Affirmations	98
Eliminating Self-Critical Thoughts	101
Celebrating Progress and Successes	104
Chapter 7: The Power of Networking	108
Identifying Networking Opportunities	109
Cultivating Meaningful Relationships	113
Effectively Utilizing Social Media	116
Understanding the Value of Mentorship	120
Chapter 8: Resilience and Adaptability	123
Building Mental Resilience	124
Embracing Change as an Opportunity	128
Developing Flexibility in Work Approaches	131
Setting Boundaries to Avoid Burnout	133
Chapter 9: Cultivating a Growth Mindset	139
Understanding Fixed vs. Growth Mindset	140
Seeking Feedback for Improvement	142
Embracing Lifelong Learning	145
Setting New Challenges for Growth	148
Chapter 10: Empowering Future Leadership	151
Developing Leadership Skills	152
Influencing with Integrity	156
Promoting Diversity and Inclusion	159
Vision Setting for Personal and Organizational Growth	161
Conclusion	164
Resources	168

Introduction

In my early days at work, I often found myself hiding in the shadows of my more confident coworkers. The office was filled with their laughter and strong voices, while I sat quietly at my desk, my heart racing at the thought of speaking up in meetings. I remember one specific project kick-off meeting where my manager asked for ideas. The room erupted with thoughts, each one louder than the last.

"Come on, Alice! What do you think?" My manager looked at me with a warm smile.

My stomach twisted in knots. My mind raced as I searched through my notes. I had ideas swirling around, but fear kept them locked away.

"I—uh, well..." My voice barely made it out, drowned out by the noise around me.

The confident ones never hesitated; they grabbed the moment with enthusiasm. They spoke as if they owned every word that came out of their mouths. Meanwhile, envy ate at me. Why couldn't I be like them? It felt like a gap separated us—one side lively and assertive, the other covered in uncertainty and self-doubt.

During breaks, I'd catch bits of their conversations—strategies and opinions shared with strong belief. I admired how easily they handled challenges and connected with higher-ups while I struggled to keep eye contact during small talk.

It was discouraging to watch them succeed while I tripped through each day. Their confidence felt out of reach, a skill set built from some hidden knowledge that I had yet to find.

As the days turned into months, I felt the weight of my hesitance bearing down on my career. Each meeting, each brainstorming session, chipped away at my ambition. I watched my colleagues rise through the ranks while I remained anchored in place, caught in a cycle of self-doubt. Promotions slipped through my fingers like grains of sand.

"Why don't you apply for that manager position?" a coworker asked one day over lunch.

I shrugged, forcing a smile. "I don't think I'm ready."

"Ready? You've been here longer than half the team!" she replied, her brow furrowing in concern.

But her words didn't ease my fears; they amplified them. Ready? I couldn't even voice my ideas during team discussions without feeling like a fraud. My mind constantly compared me to others—their confidence lit up the room while I faded into the background.

It wasn't just about missing opportunities; it impacted my salary, too. Watching others negotiate raises and benefits made me cringe. My heart raced at the thought of discussing money as if it were a forbidden topic reserved for those who had already claimed their worth.

A growing desire bubbled within me—a hunger for change that gnawed at my insides like an unfinished puzzle. I craved the ability to speak up without second-guessing every word. The more I observed, the clearer it became: I had to take control of my narrative.

"Something has to change," I whispered to myself one evening as I sat in front of my laptop, staring at job postings and articles on personal development.

That moment marked the beginning of my personal transformation journey. I sat there, staring at the screen, heart pounding and mind racing. I realized that confidence wasn't just a nice-to-have; it was essential. It shaped how others perceived me and how I navigated my role within the company.

In those early years, I watched my colleagues thrive, not just because of their skills but because they owned their voices. They took risks, shared ideas boldly, and built connections effortlessly. Their confidence opened doors—doors I felt too timid to knock on. Without it, opportunities slipped away like whispers in a crowded room.

I learned that confidence fueled motivation and engagement. It pushed professionals to embrace challenges rather than shy away from them. When you believe in yourself, tackling new projects feels less daunting; you step into your potential instead of hiding from it.

As I mulled over my hesitance that evening, I recognized this wasn't solely about career advancement. Confidence allowed for deeper connections with colleagues and helped foster a sense of belonging within the team. In every laugh shared over lunch or brainstorming session where voices echoed in unison, it became clear: those who spoke up thrived not just professionally but personally too.

I wanted that for myself—the freedom to express my thoughts without drowning in self-doubt. The spark ignited something inside me—a determination to seek out strategies that would cultivate this elusive trait and transform my narrative from one of fear to empowerment.

* * *

I eventually discovered that confidence is the very basis of professional success. It lets people take on challenges and grab opportunities without second-guessing themselves. When we tap into our confidence, we unlock our ability to inspire others and move our careers ahead.

Imagine a team that works well together—each member is brave enough to share their thoughts, leading to creative solutions. Confidence creates a space where creativity can thrive. Coworkers feel safe to share their ideas, even the out-there ones, knowing they won't be ignored or put down. This openness builds a culture of trust and respect.

When self-doubt hangs around, it not only holds back individual expression but also drags down team spirit. The room goes quiet instead of buzzing with ideas like ping pong balls. Teams get stuck, unable to change or come up with new ideas while everyone hides behind uncertainty. But when each member sees their own value, the energy changes completely.

Think about the effect of a confident leader who encourages team members to share their thoughts during meetings. Their support sparks a chain reaction—others join in, breaking free from their worries. The teamwork gains momentum; collaboration thrives as new viewpoints come forward and help everyone grow together.

Also, confidence strengthens resilience. It helps professionals handle setbacks with poise instead of panic. When self-assured people face challenges, they see them as learning chances instead of impossible barriers. This attitude spreads through teams, creating a space that accepts failure as part of the path to success.

In the end, confidence doesn't just lift careers; it changes entire workplaces into lively areas where talent grows and innovation begins. Each person's growth becomes linked to the group's success—an ecosystem thriving on shared goals and strong belief in each other's abilities.

* * *

I decided to write this book now because I wanted to share the journey that led me to where I am now, in the top management tier of a successful IT consulting company. Each lesson learned along the way carried immense weight, shaping not just my career but also my sense of self. I could finally articulate what I had gained from countless moments of struggle—those tiny victories that built upon each other to create a strong foundation.

It was time to give back. If my experiences could help even one person navigate their own path toward confidence, then it felt essential to put pen to paper. I wanted others to understand that the power of belief and small improvements could change everything—both in work and life. This book became a way for me to channel my passion for mentorship and personal growth into something tangible, something that could inspire others to believe in themselves, just as I had learned to do.

This book delves into the intricacies of building self-confidence at work, navigating the grip of impostor syndrome, and equipping you with practical techniques to improve your communication skills. I know firsthand how daunting it can feel when self-doubt creeps in, whispering that your ideas aren't worthy or that you'll never measure up.

We'll explore strategies to enhance self-esteem, focusing on recognizing your strengths and celebrating your achievements, no matter how small. Each win matters. I recall a moment when I presented a project concept during a meeting many years ago—my heart was pounding, and my palms were damp. However, the instant I noticed my colleagues nodding in approval, I felt a spark of confidence light up within me.

This journey isn't just about individual growth; it acknowledges the systemic challenges many face in the workplace. Discrimination can chip away at confidence, making it even harder to assert yourself. I've experienced this myself—those moments when being ambitious seemed to draw judgment rather than support. Together, we'll confront these realities head-on and discuss how to create environments that uplift everyone.

As we navigate these themes, I'll share actionable insights drawn from my experiences and those of others who have walked similar paths. You'll find tools designed to help you communicate effectively, manage stress, and thrive under pressure while building connections with colleagues that foster collaboration.

By understanding these dynamics and implementing the strategies we discuss, you'll gain the confidence needed to speak up and take on new challenges without hesitation.

* * *

As you turn the pages, envision yourself on a journey toward empowerment, where each chapter serves as a stepping stone toward greater self-awareness and resilience. Picture this process as if you're gearing up for a climb, each insight and strategy I share acting as your climbing gear, ready to support you through the challenges ahead.

Are you ready to embark on this transformative adventure? Each section builds upon the last, creating a tapestry of knowledge that can reshape your professional landscape. You might find yourself nodding in recognition at some stories—perhaps they mirror your own experiences with self-doubt or feeling overlooked in meetings.

Imagine integrating the techniques we discuss into your daily routine. Picture yourself entering a meeting room not just prepared but confident, sharing your ideas without hesitance. You'll discover that these small shifts—like altering how you frame your contributions—can ripple outward, impacting how others perceive you and how you see yourself.

Throughout this journey, I encourage you to reflect on your own experiences. What are the moments that challenged you? What victories have you celebrated? Each chapter will invite you to consider these questions and more, nudging you toward an enhanced understanding of your strengths and areas for growth.

Embrace this opportunity. As we navigate through strategies for overcoming impostor syndrome and building communication skills, know that every page turned brings you closer to unlocking the confidence that's been waiting within you all along.

Chapter 1: Building the Foundation of Confidence

When I first began my journey toward confidence, I didn't realize that a solid foundation was essential for success. This understanding developed in me over some period of time. Confidence isn't just a light switch you can flip on; it's a structure built brick by brick, each layer reinforcing the next. In this chapter, we'll explore how to lay that groundwork—understanding what confidence truly means and how to cultivate it in your life.

Understanding the Psychology of Confidence is our starting point. I learned early on that confidence stems from within, shaped by our beliefs and experiences. Recognizing how our thoughts influence our self-perception lays the groundwork for meaningful change.

Next, we'll dive into **Identifying Personal Strengths and Weaknesses**. It took me years to appreciate my strengths while also acknowledging areas where I could grow. Embracing this duality can feel daunting, but it's crucial for building a realistic view of ourselves.

Then comes the exciting part—**Setting Realistic and Achievable Goals**. I found that small victories paved my path to greater self-assurance. By focusing on incremental progress rather than monumental leaps, I discovered a sense of accomplishment that fueled my motivation.

Finally, we'll discuss **Developing a Positive Self-Image**. It's not just about looking in the mirror; it's about nurturing an internal dialogue that uplifts rather than diminishes. By reshaping how I spoke to myself, I began to foster an image aligned with my true potential.

Together, these elements will help us build a robust foundation for confidence that can weather any storm life throws our way.

* * *

Exploring the Psychological Aspects of Confidence

Understanding the psychology of confidence felt like uncovering a hidden map. I realized confidence isn't just an innate trait—it's a skill shaped by our experiences. Many struggle with self-doubt, often unaware of its roots. My early career reflected this; each new challenge brought overwhelming uncertainty.

I began to see how our thoughts and beliefs influence our actions. The stories we tell ourselves can empower or hinder us. Recognizing the power of my inner dialogue transformed my approach to obstacles. Instead of fixating on failures, I focused on my strengths and achievements. This shift opened avenues for growth and resilience, enabling me to face challenges directly.

Grasping the psychology of confidence was crucial in supporting others. Understanding how mindset affects performance inspired me to create an environment embracing vulnerability. By encouraging open discussions about fears and aspirations, I helped colleagues confront their insecurities. Acknowledging the psychology behind our confidence unlocks transformation potential in ourselves and those around us.

Let's get deeper into some details.

Cognitive Behavioral Approaches

Cognitive Behavioral Approaches (CBT) offer a powerful lens through which to view the connection between our thoughts, feelings, and behaviors. I often find it enlightening to consider how our self-perceptions shape our confidence levels. Many people walk around with a mental script that undermines their abilities. The first step toward change lies in recognizing that these self-perceptions can be altered with intentional effort.

By identifying negative thought patterns, we open the door to proactive change. It's about flipping the script. Instead of thinking, "I'll fail if I speak up in that meeting," we can shift to, "I have valuable insights to share." This simple reframing creates space for growth and cultivates a more resilient mindset.

Challenging irrational beliefs becomes an essential practice for boosting self-assurance. For instance, if someone believes they must be perfect to succeed, they set themselves up for failure. Embracing the idea that making mistakes is part of the learning process fosters an environment where confidence can thrive.

By actively questioning these limiting beliefs—asking ourselves if they hold true or if there's evidence to support them—we begin to dismantle the mental barriers that hinder us. Each time we confront a negative thought and replace it with a more constructive one, we strengthen our belief in ourselves.

Recognizing this dynamic between mindset and confidence inspires many to take actionable steps toward personal growth. As you start this journey, remember: reshaping your thoughts is not just about positive thinking; it's about cultivating a genuine belief in your potential and abilities.

The Role of Self-Efficacy

Self-efficacy plays a crucial role in how we approach our careers. Simply put, it's the belief in our ability to execute tasks and achieve goals. When I look at self-efficacy, I see it as the cornerstone of confidence. The stronger this belief, the better our performance and job satisfaction become.

Research consistently shows that enhanced self-efficacy translates into improved outcomes. For example, a professional who believes they can effectively lead a team is more likely to step up during crucial projects. This isn't just wishful thinking; it creates a ripple effect. When we trust in our capabilities, we take on challenges with enthusiasm, often leading to success that reinforces our self-belief.

It's essential to connect personal capabilities to measurable outcomes. Each time we meet or exceed a goal—whether it's delivering a project ahead of schedule or successfully navigating a tough conversation—we build our self-efficacy. This isn't just about one-off victories; it's about accumulating experiences that validate our skills and potential.

Moreover, embracing incremental successes fosters a growth-driven approach. It's easy to overlook small wins, but they lay the foundation for greater achievements down the line. Recognizing and celebrating these moments creates a feedback loop that boosts our confidence further.

Understanding these psychological factors is vital for anyone looking to enhance their professional journey. By cultivating self-efficacy through consistent practice and reflection, we can shift from doubt to resilience, paving the way for greater success in our careers.

CHAPTER 1: BUILDING THE FOUNDATION OF CONFIDENCE

Impact of Past Experiences

Our past experiences shape the lenses through which we view ourselves and our capabilities. Every success, every failure leaves an imprint on our confidence levels. By understanding this influence, we can begin to reframe our narratives, transforming perceived setbacks into stepping stones.

Take a moment to analyze your formative experiences. What successes stand out? Perhaps you nailed a presentation that sparked meaningful conversations or led a project that exceeded expectations. These moments of achievement hold power; they serve as reminders of your capabilities. Recognizing these instances allows you to cultivate a mindset rooted in resilience rather than fear.

On the flip side, failures also play a significant role in shaping our self-image. Many people internalize their mistakes, allowing them to define their worth. Instead of succumbing to self-doubt, it's essential to view these failures as opportunities for growth. Ask yourself: what lessons did I learn? What could I do differently next time? This reflective practice can unveil valuable insights and foster resilience, turning each setback into a lesson learned.

By identifying patterns in past achievements and failures, you empower yourself to replicate successes moving forward. Each time you recognize your progress—no matter how small—you reinforce your belief in your abilities. This process builds a solid foundation for confidence, enabling you to tackle new challenges with assurance.

Ultimately, understanding the psychological factors at play in our past experiences allows us to harness these elements intentionally. By reframing narratives around successes and failures alike, we create a resilient mindset that propels us toward future triumphs.

The Psychology of Resilience

Resilience isn't just an innate trait; it's a skill that anyone can develop over time. This understanding opens a world of possibilities. It instills hope that even in the face of setbacks, we can bounce back stronger than before. Every challenge we encounter serves as a training ground for our resilience.

Consider resilient individuals like J.K. Rowling, who faced rejection from multiple publishers before finally achieving monumental success with *Harry Potter*. Her journey underscores how persistence, coupled with belief in oneself, fosters resilience. Similarly, Oprah Winfrey's early life was fraught with challenges, yet she transformed adversity into motivation, ultimately becoming a powerful media mogul. Their stories illustrate that resilience is often born from struggle and determination.

To cultivate your own resilience strategies, start by embracing a growth mindset. Instead of viewing failures as insurmountable obstacles, see them as opportunities for learning and growth. Ask yourself what you can take away from each experience. This shift in perspective transforms setbacks into stepping stones toward success.

Another effective technique involves building a support network. Surround yourself with positive influences—friends, mentors, or colleagues who encourage you during tough times. Their perspectives can help reframe challenges and provide the encouragement needed to keep pushing forward.

Finally, practice self-compassion. When setbacks occur, treat yourself with the same kindness you would offer a friend facing difficulty. Acknowledging your feelings without judgment allows you to process experiences more effectively and regain your confidence.

By understanding these psychological factors that contribute to resilience, you can strengthen your ability to navigate challenges confidently and maintain your momentum in both personal and professional realms.

* * *

Assessing Personal Strengths and Weaknesses

Identifying personal strengths and weaknesses became a cornerstone of my journey. It wasn't just about knowing what I was good at; it was about embracing my imperfections too. When I began to recognize my strengths, I felt a spark of confidence ignite within me. Those small victories helped me build a foundation that supported my growth.

Conversely, understanding my weaknesses didn't deflate me—it empowered me. Instead of hiding from them, I learned to approach them with curiosity. For instance, public speaking had always terrified me. But acknowledging that fear allowed me to confront it head-on. I sought out opportunities to practice, each experience nudging me closer to comfort.

This process taught me the importance of self-awareness in both personal and professional settings. By identifying where I excelled and where I struggled, I crafted a path forward that felt authentic and achievable. When we recognize our strengths, we harness the power to leverage them effectively in our careers. And when we accept our weaknesses, we open ourselves up to growth and development—turning obstacles into stepping stones toward success.

Self-Assessment Tools

Structured self-assessment tools can significantly streamline the journey of self-discovery, providing an invaluable framework to help you identify your strengths and weaknesses with clarity and confidence. These assessments vary widely, encompassing everything from personality tests like the Myers-Briggs Type Indicator to comprehensive skills inventories that pinpoint specific competencies relevant to your career.

Engaging with these tools can illuminate areas where you genuinely excel. For instance, a strengths-based assessment might unveil a natural inclination toward leadership or creativity that you hadn't fully recognized before. This newfound knowledge empowers you to leverage these qualities strategically in your career. Whether it's seeking roles that align with your strengths or advocating for projects that showcase your abilities, understanding your unique attributes can propel you toward fulfilling opportunities.

On the flip side, acknowledging weaknesses can serve as a crucial launching pad for your growth efforts. Tools such as the SWOT analysis, where you evaluate your Strengths, Weaknesses, Opportunities, and Threats, encourage a comprehensive view of yourself. Instead of shying away from your limitations, facing them head-on allows you to set the stage for genuine improvement.

For instance, if public speaking ranks among your weaknesses, recognizing this through an assessment can ignite a desire to seek training or practice opportunities. Growth starts with awareness; understanding both sides of the coin equips you with actionable insights to work with. It's about creating a roadmap for personal development, where each step taken is informed by a deeper understanding of who you are and who you aspire to be. As I've learned throughout my journey, embracing both strengths and weaknesses is essential for cultivating a fulfilling professional life. Integrating self-assessment into your routine provides a structured approach to personal development. As you engage with these tools, keep in mind that this is not merely about labeling yourself but about understanding how to harness and refine your skills for future success. Each insight becomes a stepping stone toward greater self-awareness and professional growth.

Feedback From Others

Gathering feedback from others became a pivotal part of my journey toward self-awareness, shaping not only my understanding of myself but also my interactions with others. I quickly learned that soliciting insights from peers and mentors could validate my own assessments and reveal blind spots I hadn't considered. Often, we get so wrapped up in our perceptions that we overlook how others see us. By reaching out for feedback, I opened the door to a wealth of knowledge that proved invaluable in my professional growth.

When I asked colleagues about my strengths, their responses often mirrored my self-reflections but sometimes highlighted capabilities I hadn't recognized. For instance, a colleague once pointed out my knack for facilitating discussions, which helped me understand that this skill was more than just a casual talent; it was a strength worth leveraging in my role. This realization encouraged me to take on more leadership opportunities, knowing that I had a valuable skill set to contribute.

Encouraging an openness to constructive criticism also fostered a learning-oriented culture within my team. It's vital to approach feedback as an opportunity for growth rather than a personal attack. When team members felt safe sharing their perspectives, it created an environment where everyone could thrive. This culture not only enhanced our individual skills but also strengthened our collaborative spirit, leading to more innovative solutions and a greater sense of camaraderie.

Emphasizing feedback as a collaborative tool transformed how we interacted at work. Instead of viewing it as a hierarchical exchange, we approached it as a shared journey toward improvement. This shift in perspective deepened our relationships and built trust among team members, allowing us to tackle challenges more effectively and celebrate our successes together. Ultimately, this practice of seeking and embracing feedback became a cornerstone of my professional development, guiding me toward greater confidence and effectiveness in my role.

I remember one particular instance when I gathered feedback from my colleagues after leading a project kickoff meeting. I felt a mix of anticipation and dread, unsure if I had effectively conveyed my vision. When I reached out, one of my teammates, Sarah, responded with an unexpected insight.

"You really know how to get us excited about our goals," she said. "But I think you could give us more space to voice our concerns during discussions." Her honesty stung a bit at first, but as I reflected on her words, I realized she was right. I had been so eager to share my ideas that I overlooked the importance of inviting others into the conversation.

That feedback prompted me to adjust my approach in future meetings. Instead of dominating the discussion, I started asking open-ended questions, giving everyone a chance to weigh in. The change created a more collaborative atmosphere, and I noticed how it fostered richer discussions and stronger team bonds.

Another time, after facilitating a training session on effective communication, Mark approached me. "You have a great way of breaking down complex concepts," he said. "But maybe you could include more real-life examples next time to help us understand it better?" His

CHAPTER 1: BUILDING THE FOUNDATION OF CONFIDENCE

suggestion resonated deeply with me; it felt like a practical nudge toward improvement rather than criticism. Incorporating his advice into subsequent sessions not only made my presentations more engaging but also helped me connect with my audience on a deeper level. Those moments of receiving feedback transformed my perspective on growth—they turned what once felt like personal critiques into opportunities for meaningful development.

As you consider gathering feedback, remember it serves as a guide on your path to self-discovery. Actively seeking external perspectives allows you to identify strengths and weaknesses with greater clarity, ultimately paving the way for personal growth and professional development.

Reflective Journaling

Reflective journaling stands as a powerful tool for introspection, offering a dedicated space to explore personal experiences that highlight both strengths and weaknesses. When I first embraced this practice, I found that putting pen to paper transformed vague thoughts into clear insights. The act of writing provided clarity over time, revealing patterns in my behavior and thought processes that I hadn't previously noticed.

Each entry became a window into my emotional landscape. Documenting my experiences and feelings led to richer self-understanding and emotional intelligence. I began to recognize the situations that sparked joy or anxiety, which in turn helped me identify where I excelled and where I struggled. For instance, after reflecting on team meetings, I noted how my enthusiasm often energized others but also how my hesitance to ask for input sometimes stifled collaboration.

A well-maintained journal also served as a motivational reminder of progress and capabilities. On days when self-doubt crept in, flipping back through past entries showcased my journey—small victories celebrated and challenges overcome. It became evident that growth isn't linear; it ebbs and flows like the tide. This documentation not only validated my experiences but also equipped me with the knowledge to tackle new challenges head-on.

For anyone looking to enhance their self-awareness, journaling offers actionable strategies for identifying strengths and weaknesses. By consistently reflecting on daily experiences, they can cultivate a deeper understanding of themselves and leverage this knowledge for personal growth. Engaging with your own narrative provides a foundation for building confidence, ultimately guiding you toward your aspirations with clarity and purpose.

Utilizing Strengths for Professional Development

Utilizing strengths for professional development is crucial in today's competitive landscape. When we leverage our unique abilities, we enhance our value within the organization and create pathways for career advancement.

To start, identifying and understanding your strengths is the first step. Once you recognize what sets you apart, seek opportunities to apply these strengths in your daily tasks. For instance, if you excel at communication, volunteer to lead team presentations or facilitate discussions. By doing so, you not only showcase your skills but also contribute to a collaborative environment that encourages others to share their insights.

Aligning your career goals with your personal strengths fosters a sustainable path to success. This alignment ensures that your efforts resonate with what you do best, increasing job satisfaction and motivation. For example, consider Sarah, who thrived as a project manager because of her knack for organization and leadership. By

CHAPTER 1: BUILDING THE FOUNDATION OF CONFIDENCE

actively pursuing roles that required those strengths, she not only excelled in her projects but also built a reputation as a reliable leader within her organization.

Another case study involves Tom, a software developer known for his creative problem-solving abilities. He often approached challenges with innovative solutions that others hadn't considered. By sharing his unique approach during team meetings and advocating for new project ideas, Tom positioned himself as an invaluable asset to his company. His willingness to leverage his creativity not only led to successful project outcomes but also opened doors for promotions and leadership opportunities.

These examples illustrate how recognizing and harnessing individual strengths can significantly impact career trajectories. By actively seeking ways to apply our abilities in the workplace, we cultivate environments where we—and our organizations—can thrive together.

* * *

Setting Realistic and Achievable Goals

Setting realistic and achievable goals transformed my journey in ways I never anticipated. Early in my career, I often aimed too high, expecting immediate results. I envisioned myself as a confident leader overnight, which only led to frustration when reality didn't match my ambitions. It took time to realize that meaningful progress comes from breaking down big aspirations into smaller, manageable steps.

When I started setting achievable goals, everything shifted. I began with simple targets—like speaking up in meetings or leading a small project. Each success built on the last, creating a momentum that propelled me forward. These incremental wins fostered not only my confidence but also a sense of accomplishment that motivated me to tackle bigger challenges.

Moreover, realistic goals provided me with clarity and direction. Instead of feeling overwhelmed by vague aspirations, I had specific benchmarks to aim for. This structure allowed me to track my progress and celebrate each step along the way. Embracing this approach not only kept me focused but also instilled a sense of resilience; setbacks became learning experiences rather than signs of failure.

SMART Goals Framework

Setting effective goals is crucial in our journey toward success, and one of the most powerful frameworks for this is the SMART Goals criteria. The acronym stands for Specific, Measurable, Achievable, Relevant, and Time-bound. Each component plays a vital role in helping us avoid vague aspirations that can lead to frustration and, ultimately, stagnation in our personal and professional growth.

First, specificity ensures clarity in our intentions. Instead of saying, "I want to improve my public speaking," a specific goal would be, "I will deliver a presentation at next month's team meeting." This clear target not only provides focus but also establishes accountability in our achievement processes, making it easier to track our progress and identify areas for improvement.

Next comes measurability, which is essential for creating tangible indicators of progress. When we set measurable goals, we can see our development in real terms. For instance, instead of vaguely aiming to "get better at networking," we might specify, "I will connect with three new colleagues each month." This concrete approach allows us to track our efforts and celebrate small victories along the way, reinforcing our motivation and commitment.

The achievable aspect serves as a reminder to set realistic expecta-

CHAPTER 1: BUILDING THE FOUNDATION OF CONFIDENCE

tions. It's easy to dream big, but aiming for something unattainable can lead to disappointment and self-doubt. A goal like "I will lead an entire project by next quarter" might feel overwhelming if you're just starting out. Instead, consider beginning with "I will assist on a project this quarter." This gradual approach builds confidence through manageable challenges, allowing us to stretch our capabilities without feeling crushed by the weight of our ambitions.

Relevance ties our goals to our broader aspirations and ensures they align with our overall career objectives. This connection keeps us motivated and purposeful in our actions, reminding us of the bigger picture we are striving toward. Lastly, time-bound goals add an essential element of urgency. A deadline creates a sense of accountability; without it, even well-defined goals can linger indefinitely, leading to procrastination and a lack of progress.

By utilizing the SMART framework, we cultivate a results-oriented mindset that propels us toward success. Setting realistic goals becomes not just a strategy but a transformative practice on our path to building confidence and achieving our dreams. Each step we take, guided by this framework, reinforces our belief in our capabilities and paves the way for future accomplishments.

Breaking Goals into Steps

Breaking down goals into manageable steps serves as a cornerstone for maintaining motivation and building confidence throughout the journey to success. When faced with a larger objective, the prospect can feel daunting. However, by segmenting these ambitions into smaller milestones, you can prevent overwhelm and create a sense of achievement with each completed task.

Smaller milestones allow you to focus on immediate actions rather than getting lost in the enormity of the end goal. For example, if your ultimate aim is to lead a major project at work, start by identifying specific tasks such as researching project requirements or gathering input from team members. Each time you complete one of these smaller tasks, you reinforce your belief in your abilities, fostering a momentum that propels you forward.

Remember that celebrating small wins plays a crucial role in sustaining motivation. Acknowledging these achievements—whether it's finishing a report ahead of schedule or successfully facilitating a team meeting—reminds you that progress is being made. This reinforcement builds confidence, as you begin to see tangible results from your efforts.

Creating a clear action plan further aligns your goals with daily or weekly tasks, significantly increasing your chances of success. Outline what needs to be accomplished within specific time frames, breaking each task into actionable items. This structured approach not only provides direction but also allows for regular assessment of progress. By keeping your focus on what can be achieved today or this week, you ensure that you're continuously moving closer to your larger aspirations.

In summary, understanding the importance of breaking goals into smaller steps enables you to navigate their pathways to success more effectively.

Flexibility and Adaptation

Setting goals is essential, but the journey doesn't always unfold as planned. Life throws curveballs, and circumstances shift. Acknowledging that setbacks or changes in priorities are a natural part of growth keeps us motivated and resilient.

When I first began setting my professional goals, I envisioned a straight path toward success. Yet, I quickly learned that this was unrealistic. Projects would shift unexpectedly, personal commitments

CHAPTER 1: BUILDING THE FOUNDATION OF CONFIDENCE

might take precedence, or new opportunities could arise that required me to pivot. Each time I faced these changes, I realized it wasn't a failure; it was simply part of the process.

Adapting goals doesn't mean abandoning them; it means fostering resilience and maintaining a forward-looking mindset. For instance, if you initially aimed to complete a project in two months but find yourself needing more time due to unforeseen challenges, reassessing your timeline can lead to better results without sacrificing quality.

Understanding that goals evolve can be liberating. Instead of feeling defeated by changing circumstances, we can embrace them as opportunities for proactive reassessment. This mindset empowers us to adjust our expectations while still holding onto our ambitions. Perhaps you started with the intention of leading a large initiative at work but discovered your strengths lie in supporting others instead—this insight allows for valuable growth.

Incorporating flexibility into your goal-setting process enables you to navigate the twists and turns of your journey with confidence. Each adjustment becomes a stepping stone toward your ultimate aspirations, reinforcing the idea that success isn't linear but rather a dynamic path filled with learning and adaptation.

Visualizing Goals

Visualizing goals can transform aspirations into tangible possibilities. This technique strengthens your intent and belief in what you can achieve. When you picture your goals clearly, you create a mental roadmap that connects your current state with your desired outcome. The brain processes these visualizations as real experiences, which can significantly boost motivation and confidence.

One effective way to harness this power is by creating a vision board. Gather images, quotes, and symbols that resonate with your aspirations.

Arrange them on a board where you can see them daily. This visual representation serves as a constant reminder of what you're working toward, enhancing your commitment to those goals.

Mental imagery exercises also play a vital role in this process. Take time each day to close your eyes and imagine yourself achieving your objectives. Picture the details: the sounds, the emotions, the environment. As you immerse yourself in these vivid scenarios, you cultivate a sense of familiarity with success, making it feel more attainable.

Incorporating mental rehearsals further supports confidence building for planned actions. Visualize yourself executing specific tasks related to your goals—like leading a presentation or navigating a difficult conversation at work. Imagine every detail: how you'll speak, the expressions on people's faces, and how you'll handle questions or challenges that arise. This practice not only prepares you for real-life situations but also reinforces self-belief.

By utilizing visualization techniques, you empower yourself to pursue realistic goals while maintaining clarity and focus along your journey to success.

* * *

Developing a Positive Self-Image

I often found myself grappling with my self-image, especially during those early years in my career. I remember stepping into meetings, scanning the room, and feeling like an imposter among my colleagues. Developing a positive self-image became crucial not just for my confidence but for how I approached challenges at work.

When we view ourselves through a lens of positivity, it opens doors

CHAPTER 1: BUILDING THE FOUNDATION OF CONFIDENCE

to growth and opportunity. A healthy self-image fosters resilience, allowing us to bounce back from setbacks rather than dwell on failures. It encourages us to take risks, speak up in meetings, and share our ideas without fear of judgment. Over time, I learned that embracing who I was—including my quirks and imperfections—was key to unlocking my potential.

I realized that seeing myself as capable and worthy could significantly shift my interactions with others. It created a ripple effect; when I felt good about myself, I inspired those around me to do the same. They began to see me as a leader—someone who believed in their abilities—and that bolstered our team dynamic.

Developing this positive self-image required intentional effort, but the rewards were profound. It laid the foundation for not just my personal growth but also the collective success of those around me. By nurturing a supportive environment where everyone felt valued, we all thrived together.

Self-Perception vs. Reality

Many of us struggle with the gap between how we see ourselves and our actual capabilities. This discrepancy can lead to a cycle of self-doubt that hinders progress. Recognizing these gaps is the first step toward targeted self-improvement. When you identify specific areas where your perception doesn't align with reality, you can create actionable plans to enhance your skills and competencies.

For example, consider someone who believes they're not a strong presenter. They might avoid speaking up in meetings, missing opportunities to share valuable insights. In truth, their colleagues might view them as articulate and knowledgeable. By redefining your self-image based on factual accomplishments—like successfully completing a project or receiving positive feedback from peers—you can shift your perspective and bolster your confidence.

I recall a project that starkly highlighted the gap between my self-perception and reality. During a major software rollout, I led a cross-functional team. As deadlines approached, anxiety seeped in, fueling doubts about my abilities. I fixated on every misstep and stumble during presentations.

In one meeting, surrounded by talented developers, designers, and project managers, I presented our progress with a racing heart. Each glance around the room felt like judgment. When someone asked for clarification on a technical detail, panic engulfed me, and my mind went blank.

Afterward, I replayed that moment, criticizing myself for not having all the answers. Then, unexpectedly, a colleague approached me.

"You handled that really well," she said sincerely. "You led us through a tricky situation with confidence."

I was taken aback. Did she really mean that? Her perception clashed with mine, leaving me stunned; I believed I had fumbled the discussion.

That conversation was a turning point. It prompted me to reflect on my strengths and recognize that others often saw capabilities in me that I hadn't acknowledged. Rather than fixating on perceived shortcomings, I began to view feedback as a tool for growth instead of a source of shame.

To cultivate a healthier self-image, practice self-compassion. Acknowledge your achievements without downplaying them; celebrate the small wins that contribute to your growth. Surround yourself with supportive people who uplift you and challenge negative beliefs about yourself.

Understanding the influence of your environment on confidence is crucial too. Positive interactions can reinforce a healthy self-image while toxic relationships can undermine it. Pay attention to how those around you impact your perception of yourself—choose to engage with those who encourage growth and resilience.

Practicing Self-Compassion

Practicing self-compassion is vital for fostering a healthy self-image, which in turn boosts confidence and career satisfaction. When we treat ourselves with kindness, we lighten the load of unrealistic expectations that often weigh us down. Instead of striving for perfection, we can embrace our humanity—acknowledging that everyone has flaws and faces setbacks.

Self-compassion allows us to navigate challenges with resilience. Rather than beating ourselves up over mistakes, we can shift our mindset to view them as opportunities for growth. This perspective encourages learning and adaptation, transforming failures into stepping stones rather than stumbling blocks.

To cultivate self-compassion, start by speaking to yourself as you would to a friend. When you face difficulties, replace harsh self-criticism with supportive affirmations. Recognize that struggling is part of the human experience; you're not alone in feeling this way. Remind yourself that imperfection doesn't diminish your worth.

Another practical strategy involves mindfulness. Taking a moment to breathe and acknowledge your feelings without judgment can create space for compassion. This practice fosters a greater understanding of your emotional landscape and reinforces the idea that it's okay to feel vulnerable.

Surrounding yourself with positive influences also plays a crucial role in building self-compassion. Engaging with individuals who uplift and encourage you helps cultivate an environment where kindness flourishes. Their support can reinforce your self-worth and inspire you to treat yourself more gently.

By integrating self-compassion into your daily life, you'll develop a sustainable sense of worthiness that empowers you to face challenges head-on, leading to increased confidence and fulfillment in your career.

Positive Affirmations

Positive affirmations serve as powerful tools for reshaping our inner dialogue. By intentionally repeating uplifting statements, we can shift our mindset from negativity to positivity. This practice may seem simple, but it has profound effects on how we perceive ourselves and approach our daily challenges.

Creating personalized affirmations tailored to your values strengthens their impact. Think about what resonates with you—what qualities do you want to embody? Whether it's "I am capable of achieving my goals" or "I bring value to my team," these statements should reflect your true self and aspirations. The more personal and specific your affirmations, the more meaningful they become.

Integrating affirmations into your daily routine can enhance your self-confidence over time. Consider reciting them each morning as part of your ritual, perhaps while you sip coffee or prepare for the day ahead. You might write them down and place them where you'll see them frequently—on your bathroom mirror, computer monitor, or in a journal. The repetition reinforces a positive self-image, reminding you of your strengths and potential.

Research supports the notion that affirmations can significantly boost confidence levels. When you speak kindly to yourself and acknowledge your abilities, you foster a mindset open to growth and opportunity. This transformation doesn't happen overnight, but consistent practice can lead to remarkable changes in how you view yourself and interact with the world around you.

As you embrace positive affirmations, remember that nurturing a healthy self-image is essential for career satisfaction and personal fulfillment. Your thoughts shape your reality; cultivate an environment within yourself that encourages growth and resilience.

Surround Yourself with Positivity

Creating a supportive network is essential for nurturing a healthy self-image. When you surround yourself with individuals who uplift and encourage you, you foster a sense of belonging that enhances your confidence. Seek out friends, colleagues, and mentors who inspire you, challenge you to grow, and celebrate your achievements. These relationships provide a buffer against self-doubt and negativity, helping you to see your worth through their eyes.

Conversely, distancing yourself from negativity is equally important. Identify relationships that drain your energy or undermine your self-esteem. This could mean stepping back from individuals who frequently criticize or belittle you. By doing so, you create space for more positive interactions that affirm your capabilities. It's crucial to recognize that not all relationships serve your growth; some may need to be re-evaluated for your well-being.

Cultivating a positive environment goes beyond individual relationships; it encompasses the atmosphere around you. Engage in activities and communities that promote encouragement and positivity. This might involve joining groups focused on personal development or surrounding yourself with colleagues who share similar aspirations. In these spaces, you're likely to encounter shared experiences that reinforce the belief in each other's potential.

Finally, remember that modeling positivity can create a ripple effect in your network. When you practice kindness and support others in their journeys, it not only strengthens your connections but also enhances your own self-image. Positivity begets positivity; as you nurture those around you, they will likely reciprocate, further enriching the environment.

Recognizing the significance of a positive self-image will empower you to take actionable steps toward cultivating an encouraging network that uplifts both yourself and others.

Chapter 2: Overcoming Impostor Syndrome

I once sat in a conference room, surrounded by colleagues who spoke confidently, each word punctuated with assurance. As they shared their ideas, I felt like an outsider, trapped in my own head. "Who am I to contribute?" I thought, a familiar wave of self-doubt crashing over me. This feeling wasn't new; it was the insidious grip of impostor syndrome tightening around my chest. I had worked hard to reach my position, yet there I was, questioning every achievement and fearing exposure as a fraud.

Impostor syndrome is a common phenomenon, especially among high achievers like us. It manifests as an internal dialogue filled with self-doubt and fear of being "found out." It leads us to downplay our successes, attributing them to luck rather than our skills or efforts. Recognizing these signs is the first step toward overcoming this mental barrier.

In this chapter, we'll delve into the complexities of impostor syndrome. We'll start by identifying the signs that indicate you might be struggling with these feelings—those nagging thoughts that whisper you're not good enough. Then we'll analyze the root causes of this mindset, exploring how our upbringing and past experiences shape our beliefs about ourselves.

Next, we'll discuss practical strategies for breaking the cycle of self-doubt that keeps us from fully embracing our accomplishments. Lastly, we'll focus on building self-validation practices that empower you to acknowledge your worth without external validation.

Together, we will uncover the layers of impostor syndrome and develop actionable steps toward confidence and self-acceptance.

* * *

What Are the Signs of Impostor Syndrome?

Identifying the signs of impostor syndrome is crucial for anyone striving to build confidence in their professional lives. This phenomenon manifests as persistent self-doubt, feelings of inadequacy, and an overwhelming fear of being exposed as a fraud, despite evidence of competence and success. Recognizing these symptoms can be the first step toward reclaiming your self-worth and fostering a healthier mindset.

Let's dive deeper into some details.

Common Characteristics of Impostor Syndrome

Impostor syndrome often creeps into our professional lives, leaving a trail of anxiety and self-doubt. Many individuals, despite their impressive accomplishments, find themselves grappling with an overwhelming sense of inadequacy. You might look at your resume, see the awards and accolades, yet still feel like you don't belong. This disconnect creates undue stress, where every achievement feels like a stroke of luck rather than a testament to your hard work.

One of the most debilitating characteristics of impostor syndrome is the constant fear of being exposed as a fraud. This fear can stifle

CHAPTER 2: OVERCOMING IMPOSTOR SYNDROME

your ability to take risks or pursue new opportunities. You may hold back in meetings, convinced that sharing your ideas will unveil you as an imposter. Each time you hesitate to voice your thoughts, you chip away at your own potential for growth.

Perfectionism often accompanies this syndrome, leading to unrealistic expectations for yourself. You might find yourself spending excessive hours on projects, obsessing over minor details that hardly anyone else would notice. This need for perfection can become paralyzing—turning what should be an exciting challenge into an exhausting ordeal.

Recognizing these traits is essential; it marks the first step toward addressing them. Understanding that these feelings are common among high achievers can help alleviate some of the burden. Awareness allows you to confront the irrational beliefs that hold you back and begin dismantling them piece by piece.

When I began exploring impostor syndrome, I discovered a treasure trove of testimonials from professionals who bravely shared their experiences. These stories resonated deeply with me and illustrated that I was not alone in my feelings of self-doubt.

One executive recounted a moment when she received an award for her contributions to her industry. Instead of celebrating, she felt paralyzed by the fear that her peers would soon discover she didn't deserve it. "I kept thinking," she said, "that everyone else was smarter and more qualified than me. I convinced myself that my success was just luck." Hearing her story reminded me that even the most accomplished individuals grapple with similar insecurities.

Another colleague, a talented software engineer, described how he hesitated to speak up in meetings despite his extensive knowledge. "I would sit there with my heart racing, convinced that if I opened my mouth, people would see right through me," he shared. His admission revealed how impostor syndrome can stifle voices that desperately need to be heard.

Then there's the graphic designer who spent hours perfecting every detail of her work, only to find herself constantly exhausted and frustrated. "No one else cared about those tiny adjustments as much as I did," she reflected. Her journey illustrated how perfectionism can become a trap, draining energy and creativity while fueling self-doubt.

These testimonials normalize the struggle with impostor syndrome. They shine a light on shared experiences and encourage you to confront your own challenges head-on. By learning from others who have navigated similar hurdles, you gain perspective on overcoming these patterns in your life and begin to understand the signs of impostor syndrome more clearly.

Self-Assessment Tools

Self-assessment tools offer a valuable opportunity to transform the intangible feelings associated with impostor syndrome into concrete insights. These tools can take various forms, such as questionnaires, surveys, or reflection prompts designed to help you explore your thoughts and feelings about your professional capabilities.

When you sit down with a self-assessment questionnaire, you may encounter questions that ask you to reflect on your achievements, how you perceive your skills compared to your peers, or how often you doubt your qualifications. This process brings clarity to the swirling emotions of self-doubt and inadequacy that often accompany impostor syndrome. By articulating these feelings through structured questions, you start to gain a clearer understanding of your mindset.

Armed with this knowledge, you can begin taking action. For example, recognizing patterns in your responses might reveal that you often underestimate your contributions or credit external factors for your success. This awareness is crucial; it's the first step toward

CHAPTER 2: OVERCOMING IMPOSTOR SYNDROME

challenging those beliefs and reshaping how you view yourself in the workplace.

Furthermore, understanding where you stand relative to others can significantly alleviate feelings of inadequacy. Self-assessments can help highlight that many high achievers share similar fears and doubts. When you realize that these feelings are not unique to you, it can foster a sense of community and support among colleagues.

Ultimately, identifying signs of impostor syndrome through self-assessment tools empowers you to take control of your narrative and start addressing those persistent doubts. As you gather insights about yourself, you'll be better equipped to build resilience and confidence in your professional journey.

Recognizing Impact on Career

Impostor syndrome often lurks beneath the surface, quietly undermining your professional aspirations. You may not even realize how deeply it affects your career until you pause to examine its impact. Feelings of fraudulence can inhibit your job performance in significant ways. When you doubt your abilities, you might hold back during meetings or avoid taking on projects that excite you. This hesitation can prevent you from showcasing your skills, leading to missed opportunities for growth and advancement.

Acknowledging the potential career consequences of these feelings is crucial. When impostor syndrome takes hold, it can distort your perception of what success looks like and make you feel unworthy of recognition. This distortion can lead to a cycle where you strive for perfection, but any perceived failure reinforces your self-doubt. As a result, progress stalls and stagnation sets in—your ambitions feel just out of reach.

It's essential to remember that many high-achieving individuals grapple with similar impostor feelings. In fact, research indicates that around 70% of people will experience some form of impostor syndrome at least once in their lives. Recognizing that you're not alone in this struggle can provide a sense of relief and camaraderie with others who share these experiences.

By identifying the signs of impostor syndrome within yourself, you empower yourself to confront these patterns head-on. Understanding how this phenomenon can derail your career goals is the first step toward reclaiming your confidence and moving forward with purpose. When you recognize these behaviors and feelings as barriers rather than truths about yourself, you're better positioned to take action against them.

* * *

Analyzing the Root Causes

Analyzing the root causes of impostor syndrome is essential for understanding how these feelings of self-doubt take hold in our lives. This phenomenon often stems from a combination of early experiences, personality traits, and societal pressures. By identifying these underlying factors, you can begin to untangle the web of negative thoughts that contribute to your feelings of inadequacy.

Understanding the origins of impostor syndrome allows you to recognize patterns in your behavior and thinking. For instance, if you grew up in an environment that placed a high value on achievement, you might internalize the belief that your worth is tied to your accomplishments. Similarly, perfectionist tendencies can exacerbate feelings of being an impostor, as they set unattainable standards that fuel self-doubt when those standards aren't met.

CHAPTER 2: OVERCOMING IMPOSTOR SYNDROME

Moreover, recognizing external influences—like workplace culture or gender biases—can shed light on why these feelings persist. By confronting these root causes head-on, you empower yourself to challenge irrational beliefs and develop healthier perspectives about your abilities and accomplishments.

Family and Cultural Influences

Family relationships play a key role in shaping how we see ourselves and our expectations. From a young age, the messages we get from parents, siblings, and other family members can either boost our confidence or create doubt. For example, families that celebrate achievements often build a sense of pride and ability. On the other hand, if those same families focus too much on being perfect or set high standards without recognizing effort, people may come to believe that their worth depends only on their achievements.

Cultural beliefs make this situation even more complicated. Many societies promote certain ideas about success, often measured by money, status, or education. When people feel pressured to meet these expectations, they can end up feeling inadequate if they don't fit these societal norms. For instance, in cultures where academic success is very important, not doing well in school might make someone feel like a failure, no matter what unique talents or strengths they have.

Understanding how these family and cultural influences shape how you see yourself is empowering. By recognizing where your feelings of being an impostor come from—whether it's the pressure from family to succeed or societal expectations that seem impossible—you can start to challenge these beliefs. It's important to realize that many of these pressures come from outside and do not truly reflect your abilities or worth.

As you think about these influences in your life, consider how they have affected how you respond to challenges and successes. This awareness can help you reframe negative self-talk and build a healthier self-image as you move forward.

Comparison with Peers

In today's fast-paced world, it's all too easy to fall into the trap of comparing ourselves to our peers. Whether scrolling through social media or sitting in a meeting room, we often gauge our worth against the accomplishments of others. This constant comparison can reinforce feelings of inadequacy and amplify impostor syndrome.

When you see a colleague receiving praise for a project or a friend landing their dream job, it's natural to question your own achievements. "Am I doing enough?" you might wonder. "Why haven't I accomplished that?" These thoughts can spiral into self-doubt, creating an unhealthy cycle that chips away at your confidence. The truth is, such comparisons are rarely fair or accurate; they often overlook the unique paths each person has traveled.

Addressing this behavior is crucial for cultivating a healthier self-view. Instead of fixating on what others are achieving, focus on your journey. Remind yourself that everyone faces different challenges and opportunities—what may seem like an overnight success for someone else often comes after years of hard work and perseverance. Recognizing this can shift your mindset from one of envy to one of acceptance.

It's important to embrace the fact that your path is distinct from those around you. Each setback you face contributes to your growth and equips you with experiences that shape who you are as a professional. By celebrating your progress and acknowledging your unique strengths, you empower yourself to combat impostor feelings more effectively.

Understanding these dynamics behind social comparison will help illuminate the roots of your own impostor syndrome. It's a step toward confronting those underlying issues head-on and fostering self-acceptance in both your personal and professional life.

Negative Past Experiences

Negative past experiences often leave indelible marks on our self-esteem, shaping how we perceive our abilities today. A missed promotion, a poorly received presentation, or harsh feedback can create lasting impressions that linger long after the event itself. These moments can echo in our minds, whispering insidious messages of inadequacy that chip away at our confidence.

When you find yourself grappling with self-doubt, it's essential to recognize how these critiques translate into your current mindset. It's easy to internalize criticism, allowing it to morph into a narrative of failure. You might think back to a time when you stumbled during a meeting or felt unprepared for an important task, and those memories can loom large, distorting your perception of your capabilities.

Acknowledging these experiences is the first step toward redefining your narrative. Instead of letting past failures define you, consider reframing them as opportunities for growth. Each setback carries valuable lessons that can inform your approach moving forward. This process of reflection allows you to separate who you are from what has happened in the past.

As you begin this journey of exploration, keep in mind that everyone faces challenges and encounters criticism along their paths. By understanding how your negative experiences shape your feelings of impostor syndrome, you empower yourself to confront these underlying issues head-on. Embracing this awareness lays the groundwork for healing and helps cultivate a more resilient mindset that celebrates progress rather than dwelling on perceived shortcomings.

Perfectionism and Fear of Failure

Perfectionism often serves as a double-edged sword in our professional lives. While setting high standards can drive us to achieve great things, it can also create an unyielding pressure that fuels feelings of inadequacy, especially when we inevitably fall short. When you strive for perfection, any deviation from your expectations can leave you feeling like a failure. It's a vicious cycle: the higher the bar you set, the more pronounced the sense of inadequacy becomes when you don't meet it.

This connection between perfectionism and impostor syndrome runs deep. Many professionals internalize the belief that their worth is tied solely to their accomplishments. When those accomplishments don't align with their idealized version of success, self-doubt creeps in, leading to a narrative that they aren't good enough or are undeserving of their achievements. It's crucial to recognize that this mindset is not only unsustainable but detrimental to your overall well-being.

Addressing perfectionism starts with learning to forgive yourself for perceived shortcomings. Embracing the idea that no one is perfect—and that making mistakes is part of growth—can be liberating. Setting realistic expectations allows you to appreciate your progress without falling into the trap of constant self-criticism. It's about reframing how you view achievement; rather than seeing it as an all-or-nothing endeavor, understand that each step forward contributes to your journey.

Reducing the fear of failure also plays a significant role in this process. When you shift your perspective from fearing failure to viewing it as an opportunity for learning, you foster a healthier relationship with success. Recognizing that every setback provides valuable lessons can

CHAPTER 2: OVERCOMING IMPOSTOR SYNDROME

help dissolve some of those paralyzing fears, allowing you to pursue your goals with greater confidence and resilience.

Understanding these dynamics not only sheds light on your own impostor feelings but empowers you to confront them directly, setting the stage for personal growth and acceptance moving forward.

* * *

Breaking the Cycle of Self-Doubt

Breaking the cycle of self-doubt is crucial for fostering a healthy self-image and achieving professional success. Self-doubt often creates a feedback loop where negative thoughts fuel feelings of inadequacy, which in turn reinforce those same doubts. This cycle can stifle creativity, limit potential, and hinder progress in both personal and professional spheres. To break free from this cycle, it's essential to challenge irrational beliefs and replace them with affirmations that emphasize your capabilities. Recognizing past achievements and setting realistic goals can also provide a sense of accomplishment, making it easier to counter self-doubt. Taking small, actionable steps toward growth fosters resilience and encourages a more positive mindset, ultimately paving the way for increased confidence and success in your career.

Cognitive Behavioral Techniques

Cognitive Behavioral Techniques offer a powerful way to address and diminish self-doubt, particularly when it's linked to impostor syndrome. By using these methods, you can start to reshape the narrative around your abilities and build a more confident self-image.

First, consider the process of reframing unhelpful thoughts into constructive affirmations. Instead of telling yourself, "I don't deserve this job," shift that thought to "I have worked hard to be here, and I bring valuable skills to the team." This simple change in perspective helps reinforce your worthiness and capabilities. By consciously practicing positive affirmations daily, you create a mental environment that encourages growth rather than stagnation.

Next, challenge cognitive distortions—those automatic negative thoughts that arise in moments of self-doubt. Common distortions include all-or-nothing thinking, where you view situations in black-and-white terms. For instance, if you make one mistake at work, you might think, "I always mess things up." Instead, recognize this thought as an exaggeration and reframe it: "I made a mistake this time, but I've succeeded in many other projects." Challenging these distortions not only alters how you view yourself but also reinforces the idea that setbacks are part of the learning process.

Recognizing triggers for your self-doubt is another crucial step. Perhaps certain meetings or interactions with specific colleagues leave you feeling insecure. By identifying these triggers, you can craft effective counter-strategies. For example, if speaking up in meetings triggers self-doubt, prepare talking points ahead of time or practice with a trusted colleague before the meeting. Anticipating potential challenges allows you to develop responses that build your confidence rather than erode it.

Engaging in reflective journaling can further support these techniques. Documenting instances when self-doubt surfaces helps clarify patterns and offers insights into how to manage them moving forward. Over time, tracking these experiences reveals progress as well as recurring themes—allowing you to adjust your strategies as needed.

With these practical tools at your disposal, you're equipped to challenge and diminish self-doubt effectively. Fostering a more confident self-image isn't just about eliminating negative thoughts; it's about actively replacing them with affirmations that celebrate your strengths and achievements.

Goal-Setting for Success

Setting realistic and achievable goals is a powerful strategy for building confidence and diminishing self-doubt, especially when grappling with impostor syndrome. When you establish clear objectives, you create a roadmap that guides your efforts and provides structure to your journey. Instead of feeling overwhelmed by the enormity of your aspirations, breaking them down into smaller, manageable tasks makes progress feel attainable.

Start by identifying specific goals that align with your professional ambitions. Rather than declaring, "I want to be successful," focus on tangible outcomes like "I will complete this project by the end of the month" or "I will contribute at least one idea in each team meeting." These objectives offer clarity and direct your attention toward actionable steps.

As you achieve these smaller goals, you reinforce your self-efficacy—the belief in your ability to succeed. Each small win builds momentum and cultivates a sense of accomplishment that gradually chips away at feelings of inadequacy. For example, if you set a goal to present in front of your team and successfully do so, that victory becomes a building block for future presentations. Over time, as you accumulate these wins, your confidence will flourish.

It's equally important to celebrate every milestone along the way. Acknowledging progress—no matter how minor—can significantly shift your internal dialogue from self-criticism to self-appreciation. If you've managed to share an idea during a meeting or completed a task ahead of schedule, take a moment to recognize that achievement.

Maybe treat yourself to something special or simply reflect on how far you've come. These celebrations foster positivity and remind you that growth is a continuous journey.

Remember, the path to success isn't linear; setbacks are part of the process. When they occur, return to your goals as touchstones to guide you back on track. Instead of allowing a stumble to deepen feelings of self-doubt, view it as an opportunity for learning and growth. Adjusting your approach rather than abandoning your objectives helps maintain momentum and reinforces resilience.

By embracing realistic goal-setting and celebrating progress, you're not just moving toward professional success; you're also nurturing a more confident self-image capable of thriving in any environment. These practical tools empower you to challenge self-doubt effectively while paving the way for personal growth in every facet of your career.

Mentorship and Support

Finding the right mentor can be a game changer when grappling with self-doubt and impostor syndrome. Mentorship offers a unique opportunity to connect with someone who has walked a similar path and emerged stronger. These experienced individuals provide guidance, reassurance, and the wisdom of their own journeys—often filled with the same feelings of inadequacy you may experience. When I reached out to mentors during my career, their insights often illuminated paths I couldn't see on my own.

Seek mentors who resonate with your aspirations and values. Whether it's through formal programs or informal relationships, finding someone willing to share their experiences can help you realize that you're not alone in your struggles. Many successful professionals have faced self-doubt, and hearing their stories can serve as a reminder that overcoming these feelings is possible.

CHAPTER 2: OVERCOMING IMPOSTOR SYNDROME

Support networks are equally crucial. Surrounding yourself with people who believe in your potential fosters an environment where affirmations become commonplace. Colleagues, friends, and family can offer essential insights into your strengths when you find it difficult to recognize them yourself. They can also provide constructive feedback, helping you see the areas where you truly excel.

Sharing experiences within these networks can lighten the emotional load associated with impostor syndrome. Discussing feelings of inadequacy in a safe space allows for vulnerability without judgment. You'll often find that others are grappling with similar challenges; this camaraderie diminishes feelings of isolation. A simple conversation about doubts or fears can shift your perspective and help put things into context.

Engaging in collaborative projects is another effective way to diminish self-doubt. Working alongside others encourages knowledge sharing and support while allowing you to contribute your unique strengths to the group dynamic. This collaborative effort fosters accountability, making it harder to fall into negative thought patterns when surrounded by supportive peers.

As you cultivate these mentorships and support networks, remember that it's not just about receiving guidance; it's also about giving back. By sharing your own experiences and insights with others facing similar challenges, you reinforce your understanding of the journey while building connections that further strengthen your confidence.

Through mentorship and supportive networks, you can effectively challenge self-doubt and develop a more confident self-image within professional settings. The collective power of shared experiences will encourage growth not just for yourself but for those around you as well.

Mindfulness Practices

Mindfulness serves as a powerful tool for reducing self-doubt, especially when grappling with the persistent feelings associated with impostor syndrome. At its core, mindfulness promotes present-moment awareness—an essential practice that encourages us to step back from our racing thoughts and simply observe them without judgment. When we engage in mindfulness, we create a space where excessive self-judgment diminishes, allowing us to focus on the here and now.

To incorporate mindfulness into your daily routine, start by dedicating just a few minutes each day to focused breathing. Find a quiet space where you can sit comfortably. Close your eyes and take a deep breath in through your nose, allowing your chest and belly to rise. Exhale slowly through your mouth. As you breathe, pay attention to the sensation of the air entering and leaving your body. If thoughts of self-doubt creep in—like "I don't belong here" or "I'll never be good enough"—acknowledge them without attachment. Let them pass like clouds drifting across the sky. This simple exercise cultivates awareness and helps you regain control over your thoughts.

In addition to breathing exercises, practicing mindfulness techniques such as body scans can aid in stress reduction and emotional regulation. During a body scan, focus on different parts of your body, starting from your toes and moving up to your head. Notice any tension or discomfort and consciously release it with each exhale. This technique grounds you in physical sensations rather than ruminating on negative self-perceptions.

Another effective mindfulness practice is mindful journaling. Set aside time each week to reflect on your experiences without judgment. Write about moments when self-doubt surfaced—what triggered it and how it made you feel. Then, challenge those feelings by writing down counterarguments based on evidence from your achievements or feedback from colleagues. This practice empowers you to respond to self-doubt with greater clarity rather than succumbing to it.

Finally, consider integrating mindfulness into everyday activities like walking or eating. Focus entirely on the experience—notice the textures of food or the sensations of movement as you walk. By anchoring yourself in these moments, you reinforce present-moment awareness and cultivate a more confident self-image over time.

With these practical tools at your disposal, you can effectively challenge and diminish self-doubt through mindfulness practices, fostering resilience in professional settings while building a foundation for greater confidence in yourself and your abilities.

* * *

Building Self-Validation Practices

Building self-validation practices is essential for cultivating a strong sense of self-worth, particularly in professional environments where doubt often creeps in. Self-validation means recognizing and affirming your own feelings, thoughts, and achievements without relying on external approval. When you practice self-validation, you create a mental space that allows for genuine reflection on your capabilities and experiences.

To start building these practices, set aside time to acknowledge your accomplishments—big or small. This could be as simple as keeping a "success journal" where you jot down daily wins or moments when you overcame challenges. Celebrating these milestones reinforces the belief that you are capable and deserving of success.

Additionally, challenge negative self-talk by reframing critical thoughts into positive affirmations. Instead of saying, "I don't deserve this promotion," replace it with, "I have worked hard and earned this opportunity." This shift in perspective encourages a healthier dialogue with yourself.

Incorporating mindfulness techniques can also enhance self-validation. Take moments to breathe deeply and check in with your feelings throughout the day. Ask yourself what emotions arise during different situations at work—recognizing these feelings can validate your experiences and help you understand their origins.

Daily Reflection Exercises

Creating habits that reinforce self-acceptance and confidence is crucial for professional growth. One of the most effective practices is journaling. This simple yet powerful tool allows individuals to articulate their thoughts and feelings, providing much-needed clarity in a world often filled with noise and distractions.

When you sit down to journal, you create a dedicated space to unpack your experiences. It's a moment to pour out everything swirling in your mind, from frustrations about work to celebrations of small victories. As you write, the jumble of emotions starts to settle. You begin to see patterns and themes in your thoughts, which can illuminate areas for personal growth or reinforce the strengths you already possess.

Moreover, reflecting on accomplishments nurtures a deeper appreciation of your achievements. In the hustle of daily life, it's easy to overlook what you've done well. Journaling serves as a reminder of your progress, whether it's completing a challenging project or receiving positive feedback from a colleague. Each entry becomes a snapshot of your journey, capturing moments when you overcame obstacles or made significant strides forward.

This practice helps build a stronger self-narrative over time. As you

CHAPTER 2: OVERCOMING IMPOSTOR SYNDROME

document your experiences and accomplishments, you start to weave together a story that emphasizes resilience and capability. Instead of focusing solely on setbacks or challenges, your narrative transforms into one that celebrates growth and perseverance. This shift in perspective can be incredibly empowering; it reinforces the belief that you are more than capable of navigating whatever comes your way.

To get started with journaling for self-reflection, set aside time each day—whether it's five minutes or half an hour—to write without judgment. Consider prompts like "What went well today?" or "What challenges did I overcome?" These questions guide your reflection and encourage you to acknowledge both the big wins and the small victories.

Incorporating daily reflection exercises into your routine not only enhances self-acceptance but also fosters confidence. By regularly affirming your achievements through writing, you cultivate an empowered mindset that propels you forward in both your personal and professional life.

Positive Affirmations

Creating a habit of positive affirmations can be a powerful tool for fostering self-acceptance and building confidence. Daily affirmations encourage a shift from negative self-talk to positive reinforcement, which can drastically alter how you perceive yourself and your capabilities. Instead of letting self-doubt dictate your thoughts, affirmations help you reclaim your narrative.

To start, consider what triggers your self-doubt. Identify specific situations or thoughts that undermine your confidence—maybe it's during meetings when you hesitate to share ideas or when facing deadlines that feel overwhelming. Once you recognize these triggers, craft empowering statements that directly address them. For instance, if you often think, "I'm not good enough to lead this project," replace it with, "I bring valuable insights and experience to my team." Tailoring affirmations in this way makes them more relevant and impactful.

Consistency is key in using affirmations effectively. Try incorporating them into your daily routine—perhaps recite them each morning as you prepare for the day ahead or write them down in a journal before bed. This regular practice nurtures a supportive internal dialogue, allowing these positive statements to become ingrained in your mindset over time. The more frequently you reinforce these beliefs, the more likely they are to take root in your subconscious.

Another effective technique is to create visual reminders of your affirmations. Write them on sticky notes and place them around your workspace or home—on mirrors, computer screens, or even inside cabinet doors where they're easily visible throughout the day. Each time you encounter these reminders, take a moment to pause and internalize the message.

You might also experiment with saying affirmations aloud. Speaking these empowering statements can elevate their impact and reinforce their meaning. Find a quiet space where you feel comfortable expressing yourself without hesitation; let the words resonate as you speak them into existence.

Remember, the goal of using positive affirmations isn't just to mask insecurities but to genuinely cultivate an inner sense of strength and resilience. As you embrace this practice consistently, you'll find yourself navigating challenges with newfound assurance and clarity.

By adopting these strategies for creating and utilizing positive affirmations, you're not only setting yourself up for success but also nurturing a profound sense of self-worth that will serve as a solid foundation for your personal and professional journey.

Setting Boundaries

Establishing personal and professional boundaries is essential for nurturing self-acceptance and confidence. Recognizing your limits allows you to protect your mental health, ensuring you don't overextend yourself in situations that could lead to burnout or heightened self-doubt. When you clearly define what is acceptable and what is not, you create a foundation that reinforces your self-worth.

Understanding your boundaries means acknowledging when something feels uncomfortable or overwhelming. It's about tuning into your own needs and being honest with yourself about what you can handle. This practice becomes even more crucial in environments where external pressures can amplify impostor feelings. When demands from colleagues, superiors, or clients pile up, it's easy to slip into the mindset of thinking you need to prove your worth by saying yes to everything. But the truth is, stretching yourself too thin can diminish your performance and reinforce those nagging feelings of inadequacy.

Setting boundaries protects against these pressures. It empowers you to say no without guilt, fostering an environment where you can thrive rather than merely survive. For example, if a colleague asks for help on a project but you're already overwhelmed with your responsibilities, a polite refusal isn't just an option; it's necessary for maintaining your well-being. By establishing this boundary, you signal respect for both yourself and your workload.

Moreover, this practice encourages self-respect and personal agency in how you react to others' expectations. Setting boundaries communicates that you value your time and energy; it also teaches those around you how to treat you. You become an advocate for yourself rather than a passive participant in decisions affecting your life.

In practical terms, begin by identifying areas in which you feel stretched too thin—whether it's work commitments, social obligations, or family expectations. Then consider the changes needed to protect your mental space. Write down specific boundaries you'd like to implement and commit to them as if they were non-negotiable tasks on your calendar.

Remember, setting boundaries isn't about shutting others out; it's about creating a safe space where you can recharge and operate at your best. By doing so, you'll cultivate resilience against negative influences that threaten your confidence and sense of self-worth.

By embracing these strategies for setting personal and professional boundaries, you're taking actionable steps toward fostering a more empowered and confident self.

Engaging in Self-Care

Engaging in self-care is more than just a trendy buzzword; it's a vital practice that fosters confidence and resilience, particularly against the challenges of impostor syndrome. When you prioritize personal well-being, you build a foundation that enables you to navigate the pressures of work and life with greater ease.

To start, recognize that self-care routines help you value yourself beyond your professional labels. Often, we tie our identities to our careers, leading to a narrow view of our worth. When we embrace self-care—whether it's setting aside time for exercise, enjoying a hobby, or simply taking moments to relax—we send a clear message: our value isn't solely defined by job titles or accolades. Engaging in activities that nourish your spirit allows you to reconnect with who you are outside the workplace, enhancing your overall sense of self-worth.

Connecting self-care to confidence means understanding that holistic wellness is essential for thriving both personally and professionally. When you care for your mental and physical health, you're better equipped to face challenges head-on. For instance, regular exercise not only boosts your mood but also increases energy levels and sharpens focus. This enhanced state can empower you during meetings or presentations, helping to quiet those nagging doubts that often accompany impostor syndrome.

Moreover, incorporating mindfulness practices into your self-care routine can create significant shifts in how you perceive yourself. Mindfulness encourages you to be present in the moment, fostering acceptance of your thoughts and feelings without judgment. This practice helps reduce anxiety and cultivates resilience against negative self-talk—key components of impostor syndrome.

Remember that self-care isn't selfish; it's an investment in yourself. By dedicating time each day or week for activities that recharge and uplift you, you're actively reinforcing the belief that you deserve care and respect. This mindset can translate into greater confidence in your abilities at work and beyond.

By embracing these self-care strategies, you're not just nurturing your well-being; you're laying the groundwork for a more empowered and confident version of yourself.

Chapter 3: Enhancing Communication Skills

In my early days in HR department, I often found myself stumbling through conversations, wishing for a magic wand that could transform my clumsy words into articulate expressions. I didn't just want to communicate; I wanted to connect. But instead, I often left meetings feeling as though I'd just blurted out incoherent thoughts, hoping someone understood what I meant.

During my career path in the corporate IT world, I realized that effective communication is a cornerstone of successful collaboration and relationship-building. The ability to convey ideas clearly can make or break projects, influence team dynamics, and ultimately shape careers. So, how do we refine our communication skills to enhance our professional lives?

First on the agenda is *practicing active listening*. This isn't merely hearing words; it's about engaging with the speaker. In conversations, especially in meetings where opinions clash or discussions heat up, I learned to focus on understanding others' perspectives rather than waiting for my turn to speak. By honing this skill, I discovered that acknowledging others fosters an environment of trust and respect—essential ingredients for any productive workplace.

Next up is *articulating thoughts clearly and confidently*. During team presentations and meetings, I would often catch myself second-

CHAPTER 3: ENHANCING COMMUNICATION SKILLS

guessing my contributions. But over time, with practice and intentionality, I learned techniques to express ideas with clarity. The goal wasn't just to speak but to ensure my message resonated with colleagues. When you believe in what you're saying and convey it confidently, people listen—and more importantly, they engage.

Then there's the often-overlooked aspect of **understanding nonverbal cues**. A simple nod or a furrowed brow can tell you more than words ever could. As I navigated different teams and cultures within my career, recognizing these signals became vital for gauging reactions and adjusting my responses accordingly.

Lastly, adapting communication styles is crucial for effective collaboration. Not everyone processes information in the same way; some prefer detailed data while others thrive on big-picture thinking. By being mindful of these differences and flexibly adjusting my approach based on the audience at hand, I've fostered stronger relationships within teams.

This chapter dives deeper into these elements of communication that have transformed not only how I interact with others but also how those interactions influence outcomes at work.

* * *

Practicing Active Listening

Active listening stands as a cornerstone of effective communication, especially in the workplace. It requires more than just hearing words; it demands full concentration and engagement. When you practice active listening, you truly absorb what the speaker is conveying. This foundational skill fosters understanding and builds trust among colleagues, leading to more productive interactions.

Understanding Active Listening

To grasp the essence of active listening, we must first recognize its components. Active listening involves fully concentrating on the speaker, understanding their message, responding thoughtfully, and retaining the information shared. When you engage in this process, you cultivate a genuine connection with the person speaking.

Effective communication starts with truly hearing the speaker. Imagine a colleague sharing their thoughts during a brainstorming session. If your mind drifts to your upcoming tasks or your phone buzzes with notifications, you miss critical nuances of their message. By actively listening, you not only grasp the content but also understand the emotion behind it—creating an opportunity for rapport.

This practice builds trust in professional relationships. When colleagues feel heard and valued, they are more likely to express their ideas openly. Conversely, neglecting active listening can lead to misunderstandings and conflicts that stifle collaboration.

Barriers to Active Listening

However, practicing active listening isn't without its challenges. Common distractions—like multitasking or personal biases—can hinder your ability to engage fully in conversations. Multitasking might seem efficient on paper; yet when you're trying to divide your attention between a meeting and your email inbox, you're likely missing vital cues from the speaker.

Personal biases can also cloud comprehension. For instance, if you enter a discussion with preconceived notions about someone's ideas or background, it becomes difficult to remain open-minded. Acknowledging these biases is crucial; by doing so, you enhance your capacity for understanding.

CHAPTER 3: ENHANCING COMMUNICATION SKILLS

Being aware of distractions allows you to minimize them during conversations. Set aside electronic devices when possible; this small act can significantly elevate your focus and signal to others that their words matter.

Additionally, strategies like note-taking can keep you engaged in discussions. Writing down key points not only reinforces your memory but also demonstrates to the speaker that you are invested in what they're saying.

Techniques for Enhancing Active Listening

Once you've acknowledged barriers to active listening, it's essential to explore techniques that enhance this skill further. Two effective methods are paraphrasing and asking clarifying questions.

Paraphrasing involves restating what you've heard in your own words—a powerful way to show the speaker that you're engaged and validating their thoughts. For example, if a colleague shares concerns about project deadlines, paraphrasing their statement back can reinforce that you've understood: "So you're feeling overwhelmed by the upcoming deadlines and think we should adjust our timeline?" This simple act creates an atmosphere where open dialogue thrives.

Asking clarifying questions serves a similar purpose by promoting deeper conversations and enhancing clarity. If something isn't clear during discussions—perhaps technical jargon is used—don't hesitate to ask for elaboration. Phrases like "Can you explain that further?" or "What do you mean by...?" encourage speakers to share more information while ensuring everyone is on the same page.

These practices contribute significantly to creating a positive communication environment within teams. Colleagues feel respected when they know their thoughts are not just heard but genuinely considered and understood.

Active Listening in Diverse Environments

As workplaces become increasingly diverse, adapting listening strategies in cross-cultural settings ensures inclusivity—a vital aspect of team dynamics today. Understanding cultural differences enhances mutual respect among team members who may come from varying backgrounds with unique communication styles.

For example, some cultures may prioritize directness while others emphasize subtlety or indirect communication cues. Being mindful of these differences enriches overall communication experiences and fosters stronger teamwork.

In diverse environments, it's also essential to be aware of non-verbal cues—such as body language or facial expressions—that can provide context beyond spoken words. Someone's crossed arms might signal defensiveness or discomfort; recognizing such signals allows for timely adjustments in conversation dynamics.

Inclusivity through active listening encourages stronger collaboration among team members by validating everyone's voice within group settings—a necessity for innovation-driven organizations seeking diverse perspectives.

By applying these techniques—practicing active listening while navigating barriers and adapting approaches based on cultural contexts—you empower yourself with invaluable skills that enhance workplace interactions.

Ultimately, developing active listening skills is not merely an exercise but an essential investment into fostering effective communication and building stronger professional relationships across teams.

* * *

CHAPTER 3: ENHANCING COMMUNICATION SKILLS

Articulating Thoughts Clearly and Confidently

Articulation isn't just about speaking; it's about making your thoughts accessible to others. In the workplace, clear and confident articulation serves as a bridge between ideas and understanding. It transforms concepts into actionable insights, enabling teams to collaborate effectively and drive projects forward.

Clarity in Communication

When I consider clarity in communication, I think about the last presentation I gave on a complex project we had been working on. Initially, my slides brimmed with industry jargon and technical terms that left some team members scratching their heads. As I glanced around the room, I could see confusion creeping onto faces, and that's when it hit me—difficult jargon obscures messages.

If the goal is to convey ideas effectively, simplicity is paramount. Using straightforward language enhances engagement. If you present ideas in a convoluted manner, listeners may disengage or misunderstand key points. Simplifying your language allows your audience to grasp concepts quickly, promoting a sense of inclusion in discussions.

Clarity promotes confidence—not only in the speaker but also in the listener. When people understand what you're saying, they feel empowered to contribute their own thoughts or ask questions for further clarification.

The Role of Confidence

Confidence plays an equally crucial role in how our messages are perceived. Think back to a time when you were captivated by a speaker—their tone resonated with authority and conviction. A confident tone instills trust; it suggests that the speaker believes in their message, which compels listeners to pay attention.

Your body language can complement verbal communication significantly. Standing tall with open gestures conveys assurance without uttering a word. Maintaining eye contact builds rapport with your audience and reinforces your commitment to what you're saying. Together, these elements create an atmosphere of respect—both for yourself and your audience.

Self-belief can transform communication experiences from ordinary to impactful. It enables you to deliver your message with enthusiasm and energy, making it more memorable for those who hear it.

Practical Techniques for Articulation

Preparing for impactful interactions involves practical techniques that enhance clarity and reduce anxiety. Outlining key points before engaging in conversation is one of the simplest yet most effective methods I've employed throughout my career.

By structuring my thoughts ahead of time, I avoid getting lost in details or tangents during discussions. This preparation increases clarity—my points flow logically from one to another—and ultimately cultivates a more meaningful exchange.

Practice is another vital component of clear articulation. Just like athletes train before a game or musicians rehearse before a concert, honing your delivery can make all the difference in how well you communicate your message.

Consider rehearsing speeches or presentations aloud—preferably in front of someone you trust who can offer constructive feedback. The more comfortable you become with your material, the more natural your delivery will feel during actual interactions.

Tailoring Messages for Various Audiences

One size does not fit all when it comes to workplace communication; tailoring messages for different audiences enhances comprehension significantly. Understanding your audience helps you choose appropriate vocabulary and adjust your tone accordingly.

For example, if I'm presenting to senior executives who may be pressed for time, I prioritize high-level summaries over intricate details. Conversely, if I'm discussing technical matters with my design team, using industry-specific terms makes sense since they have the background knowledge needed for deeper conversation.

Flexibility in style accommodates diverse listeners within any group setting as well; adapting language based on who you're addressing ensures everyone feels included in discussions while still receiving pertinent information.

Audience awareness strengthens the impact of your message because it shows respect for their perspective—demonstrating that you value their input encourages engagement across various levels within an organization.

In sum, mastering clear and confident articulation is essential for effective workplace communication. By emphasizing clarity through simple language choices while embodying confidence through both verbal cues and body language techniques, we foster meaningful exchanges that propel our ideas forward while building connections among colleagues along the way.

Whether it's preparing key points ahead of time or adapting our messages based on specific audiences' needs—each step taken toward improving articulation contributes significantly toward becoming not just better communicators but also empowered professionals ready to tackle any challenge that arises in our careers together!

Understanding Non-Verbal Cues

Non-verbal communication encompasses the myriad ways we express ourselves without uttering a single word. It includes body language, facial expressions, gestures, and even the use of space. As I advanced professionally, I learned that understanding non-verbal cues significantly enhances interpersonal interactions in the workplace. Let's explore why these signals matter and how they can transform your communication effectiveness.

Importance of Non-Verbal Cues

Non-verbal cues can either reinforce or contradict verbal messages. Picture this: you're delivering a presentation, and while your words convey enthusiasm about a project, your crossed arms and downcast eyes tell a different story. This disconnect can create confusion for your audience, leaving them unsure of your true feelings. When our verbal and non-verbal messages align, we establish clarity and build trust.

Being aware of non-verbal cues doesn't just improve communication; it fosters stronger relationships with colleagues. It's crucial to remember that misinterpretation of these signals can lead to unnecessary conflicts. For instance, if someone appears disinterested during a discussion—perhaps leaning back with their arms crossed—you might assume they disagree with your ideas when they're simply tired or distracted by external factors.

CHAPTER 3: ENHANCING COMMUNICATION SKILLS

Types of Non-Verbal Communication

Different types of non-verbal communication convey various messages. Take posture as an example. Open body language—standing tall with shoulders back—signals receptiveness and engagement. Conversely, slumped shoulders might indicate disinterest or lack of confidence.

Eye contact is another powerful tool in the realm of non-verbal communication. Making eye contact fosters connection; it demonstrates sincerity and shows that you value the other person's perspective. However, excessive eye contact can feel intimidating, so balance is key.

The way we utilize space also influences comfort levels during conversations. Standing too close may invade personal space and make someone uncomfortable, while standing too far away could signal detachment or aloofness. Recognizing how to navigate physical proximity is essential for effective interaction.

Interpreting Non-Verbal Signals

Understanding context is paramount when interpreting non-verbal cues correctly. The cultural background and situational aspects surrounding an interaction play significant roles in shaping these signals. For example, while direct eye contact may be considered a sign of respect in some cultures, it might be viewed as confrontational in others.

Additionally, recognizing inconsistencies between verbal and non-verbal cues is vital for effective communication. If someone says they're "fine" but their clenched fists betray anger or frustration, taking note of this incongruence allows you to respond appropriately rather than taking their words at face value.

Sensitivity to non-verbal signals cultivates empathy and understanding within the workplace. When we learn to interpret these cues accurately, we become better equipped to address our colleagues' needs effectively.

Improving Your Non-Verbal Skills

Practicing awareness of your own non-verbal cues can dramatically improve communication effectiveness. Self-regulating body language enables you to project confidence and openness in any interaction—a critical component in leadership roles or team dynamics.

Regular self-reflection on your non-verbal tendencies promotes growth over time. Ask yourself: Do I maintain eye contact during conversations? Am I aware of my posture? Taking stock of these elements allows for conscious adjustments that enhance how others perceive you.

Feedback from peers can also foster improvement in your non-verbal skills. Consider asking trusted colleagues if they notice any patterns in your body language or facial expressions during meetings or discussions; their insights could provide valuable perspective on how to refine your approach further.

In conclusion, honing our understanding of non-verbal communication opens up new pathways for more profound connections with our colleagues and superiors alike—and elevates our ability to navigate complex professional environments successfully!

* * *

CHAPTER 3: ENHANCING COMMUNICATION SKILLS

Adapting Communication Styles

In the workplace, effective communication can make or break relationships. The way we express ourselves and interact with others influences not just our individual effectiveness, but also team dynamics as a whole. Understanding how to adapt our communication styles is crucial for fostering a collaborative and productive environment.

Identifying Your Communication Style

Awareness of your personal communication style is the first step toward improvement. Everyone has a natural way of conveying thoughts and emotions, and recognizing this can significantly enhance relational dynamics.

What's your default mode of communication? Are you direct and to the point, or do you prefer a more conversational approach? Perhaps you lean towards being analytical, focusing on data and facts, or maybe you're more expressive, relying on emotions and narratives to convey your messages.

Understanding these traits allows you to pinpoint your strengths—like being able to drive results through concise messaging—or areas where you might struggle. For instance, if you're naturally more reserved, initiating conversations might feel daunting. Regular self-assessment can clarify your preferences and help you identify which aspects of your style may require refinement.

This self-awareness can empower you to approach conversations with confidence, ensuring that your unique style complements rather than hinders your interactions with others.

Recognizing Others' Styles

While understanding your own communication style is vital, recognizing the styles of those around you is equally important. Observing how colleagues express themselves can provide insight into their preferences, allowing you to tailor your interactions for better outcomes. Take note of their verbal and non-verbal cues during meetings or casual discussions. Do they respond better to detailed explanations or quick summaries? Are they open to back-and-forth dialogue or do they prefer straightforward instructions?

By identifying these patterns in others' communication styles, you can adapt your approach accordingly. For example, if a teammate seems overwhelmed by too much information at once, consider simplifying your message or breaking it down into digestible parts. Flexibility in communication leads to smoother conversations and fosters stronger teamwork.

Recognizing different styles not only enhances individual interactions but also contributes positively to overall team dynamics. When everyone feels understood and valued in their preferred method of communication, collaboration flourishes.

Techniques for Adapting

Once you've identified both your style and those of others, it's time to put that knowledge into practice through specific techniques designed for adapting effectively.

One useful method is mirroring—subtly mimicking the other person's body language or speech patterns during a conversation. This technique can create a sense of familiarity and comfort between participants. If someone leans in while speaking enthusiastically about an idea, leaning in yourself shows engagement and encourages them to share more freely.

Open communication is another essential element when adapting styles. By fostering an environment where team members feel safe expressing their thoughts and preferences openly, everyone benefits from honest exchanges that inform better practices moving forward. Consider starting conversations with prompts like: "How do you prefer we communicate about project updates?" This invites input while establishing rapport.

Seeking constructive feedback also plays a critical role in enhancing adaptability. After important discussions or presentations, ask colleagues for their perspectives on what worked well or what could be improved regarding how you conveyed information. Feedback helps refine not only your style but also fosters an atmosphere of growth within the team.

Challenges in Adapting

Navigating different communication styles can present its own set of challenges. Misinterpretations often arise from mismatched styles; what feels straightforward for one person may come across as brusque or dismissive to another.

Being aware of these potential pitfalls helps create opportunities for finding common ground amidst diversity in communication preferences. Take time to clarify any misunderstandings right away; if something doesn't resonate as intended during an exchange, address it head-on rather than allowing confusion to fester.

Another challenge lies in managing one's emotional response when faced with differing styles that clash with personal preferences. It's easy to feel defensive if someone critiques our approach—especially if we're passionate about our method! Practicing patience during these moments enables us not only to absorb constructive criticism but also encourages mutual respect among team members regardless of varying styles.

Strategies for overcoming differences include maintaining an open mindset toward new ideas while respecting diverse perspectives within the group dynamic; acknowledging that adaptability requires effort from all involved parties ultimately strengthens collaboration efforts across teams!

By prioritizing adaptability through self-awareness alongside keen observations about colleagues' preferences—and implementing effective techniques—teams will cultivate positive environments ripe for innovation driven by harmonious exchanges between individuals committed both personally and collectively towards success!

Chapter 4: Thriving Under Pressure

Navigating the daily demands of a professional environment can feel like walking a tightrope. As deadlines loom and expectations soar, stress often becomes an unwelcome companion. I remember moments when the pressure seemed insurmountable, leaving me breathless and unsure of how to keep my balance. Yet, through my experiences, I learned that thriving under pressure isn't just about enduring—it's about developing practical techniques to not only survive but also flourish.

In this chapter, I will share strategies that transformed my approach to high-stress situations. We'll dive into managing time effectively, ensuring that every minute counts and alleviates the feeling of being overwhelmed. Stress-reduction techniques will provide tools to maintain composure and clarity when stakes are high.

You'll discover how to prioritize tasks under pressure, allowing you to focus on what truly matters amidst the chaos. Lastly, we'll explore learning from failure—a vital aspect of growth that often gets overlooked but holds invaluable lessons for resilience. Together, these insights can empower you to turn stressful circumstances into opportunities for personal and professional growth.

* * *

Managing Time Effectively

In the high-pressure world of professional life, managing time effectively becomes a lifeline. When tasks pile up and deadlines loom, the chaos can quickly spiral into overwhelm. However, implementing strategic time management techniques not only reduces stress but also enhances productivity. Let's delve into some essential methods to help you take control of your time and thrive even in demanding situations.

Prioritization Techniques

The first step in effective time management is learning to prioritize tasks. Not all tasks carry the same weight; some have more significant impacts on your goals than others. Understanding the distinction between urgent and important tasks is crucial.

Urgent tasks demand immediate attention—think of emails that require quick responses or last-minute requests from your manager. On the other hand, important tasks contribute to long-term success but may not feel as pressing in the moment. By identifying which tasks fall into these categories, you can focus on what truly matters.

For instance, if you're faced with an impending deadline for a project that aligns with your team's strategic objectives, prioritize that over responding to an email that can wait. This approach alleviates pressure by ensuring you tackle high-impact work first.

Effective prioritization leads to greater achievement while reducing feelings of overwhelm. Concentrating on significant goals instead of getting lost in trivial details makes a world of difference.

Creating Structured Schedules

Once you've prioritized your tasks, the next step is crafting a structured schedule. A well-organized approach fosters a sense of control and significantly reduces anxiety.

Time Blocking

Time blocking is one effective technique for creating structure in your day. This method involves dedicating specific blocks of time to particular activities or types of work. For example, set aside two hours each morning for focused project work without distractions before jumping into meetings or responding to emails.

This technique encourages focused work and helps mitigate interruptions since you're clear about when you're available for other commitments versus when you're deep in concentration on a task at hand.

Utilizing Tools and Apps

In today's digital age, countless tools and apps can streamline planning efforts and enhance accountability. Applications like Trello or Asana allow you to organize projects visually, track progress, and set reminders for upcoming deadlines.

By leveraging technology to create structured schedules, you free up mental space previously occupied by worries about forgetting important dates or missing out on vital tasks.

Setting Realistic Deadlines

Deadlines can either motivate or suffocate us depending on how we approach them. Setting realistic deadlines improves task flow and encourages sustained productivity without risking burnout.

It's essential to understand personal limits when establishing timelines for completion. Overcommitting leads only to frustration when expectations exceed capacity; therefore, assess how long similar past projects took before determining new deadlines.

Encouraging realistic timelines cultivates sustained productivity while preventing feelings of overwhelm associated with impossible targets. You'll find that clearly communicating expectations with colleagues further eases stress during collaborative projects as everyone remains aligned on achievable outcomes.

For instance, instead of committing to finish a report by tomorrow—when it typically takes three days—set an appropriate deadline based on historical data gathered from similar projects or consult team members who may have insights into how long certain deliverables usually require.

Reviewing and Adjusting Plans

Finally, flexibility plays a critical role in effective time management. Regularly reviewing plans allows for necessary adjustments that reflect changing priorities or unexpected challenges that arise throughout the day.

When faced with obstacles—be it unforeseen responsibilities at work or personal emergencies—being adaptable ensures that you continue moving forward rather than succumbing entirely to stress-induced paralysis. Reassessing daily goals can also foster resilience against pressure situations since it allows room for modifications based on evolving needs.

Consider setting aside a few minutes each week dedicated solely to reviewing progress against your goals; ask yourself what worked well this past week? What didn't? Did unexpected challenges hinder any efforts? By identifying patterns during these reflections enables better

CHAPTER 4: THRIVING UNDER PRESSURE

preparation moving forward into subsequent weeks' schedules without losing momentum towards achieving larger objectives overall.

The ability to pivot plans while maintaining focus provides reassurance that progress doesn't have to stall despite disruptions along our paths toward success; flexibility becomes our ally rather than an enemy when times get tough!

By implementing these essential time management techniques—prioritization strategies designed around identifying significant goals first; creating structured schedules using tools like time blocking alongside helpful apps; setting realistic deadlines based upon honest assessments regarding personal limits followed by regular reviews enabling timely adjustments—you'll cultivate efficiency amidst chaos while minimizing overwhelming feelings often experienced during high-pressure environments!

* * *

Utilizing Stress-Reduction Techniques

Navigating the high-pressure environment of the workplace can feel like walking a tightrope, where every step requires balance and focus. Stress has a way of creeping in when you least expect it, but the good news is that there are practical techniques to help you manage that stress effectively. Let's explore some actionable strategies that can enhance your resilience and allow you to thrive even in the most demanding situations.

Mindfulness and Meditation

One of the most effective methods for reducing stress is mindfulness. This practice encourages us to remain present and fully engaged with the current moment rather than being swept away by worries about the past or future.

Engaging in mindfulness enhances focus and decreases anxiety. By directing your attention to what's happening right now, you can interrupt cycles of negative thought patterns. Simple practices, such as taking a moment to observe your surroundings or focusing on your breath, can help ground you in reality.

Short meditation sessions offer another powerful way to reset mental clarity amid chaos. Just a few minutes of deep breathing or guided meditation can provide an invaluable mental break. Apps like Headspace or Calm offer quick sessions tailored for busy professionals, making it easier than ever to incorporate mindfulness into your routine.

Implementing mindfulness fosters a more resilient mental state during stressful situations. As you practice being present, you'll find that you respond more calmly to challenges rather than reacting impulsively out of fear or anxiety.

Physical Activity

Another potent tool for stress management lies in physical activity. Regular exercise acts as a powerful remedy for tension and fatigue. When you move your body—whether through running, dancing, yoga, or simply taking a brisk walk—your brain releases endorphins, chemicals that promote feelings of happiness and euphoria.

Engaging in physical activities provides not only an outlet for pent-up energy but also an opportunity to clear your mind. Exercise serves as a natural antidote to stress; even just 20 minutes of moderate activity

CHAPTER 4: THRIVING UNDER PRESSURE

can help elevate your mood and sharpen your focus.

Encouraging short movement breaks throughout the day can rejuvenate energy levels during long work hours. If you feel overwhelmed by deadlines or meetings piling up, step outside for some fresh air or stretch at your desk for a minute or two. These small bursts of movement disrupt monotony while providing valuable moments of reprieve from tension.

Breathing Exercises

Intentional breathing techniques offer yet another method to diffuse stress quickly. Practicing deep breathing promotes relaxation by signaling your body to shift from fight-or-flight mode back into a state of calm.

A simple technique involves inhaling deeply through your nose for a count of four, holding that breath for another four counts, then exhaling slowly through your mouth over six counts. Repeat this cycle several times until you notice a reduction in tension.

These breathing exercises can be employed swiftly during moments when stress feels overwhelming. They don't require any special equipment—just find a quiet spot if possible and dedicate two minutes to focusing solely on your breath. This practice anchors attention away from racing thoughts while grounding you back into the present moment.

By incorporating deep breathing into your daily routine—whether at the start of each day or between tasks—you equip yourself with tools needed to manage rising levels of stress effectively.

Cultivating a Supportive Environment

Finally, don't underestimate the power of community when it comes to mitigating workplace stress. Building a network of supportive colleagues fosters an environment where individuals feel valued and understood during tough times.

Encouraging open communication reduces feelings of isolation that often accompany high-pressure situations. When team members openly share their experiences—whether they're successes or challenges—it creates an atmosphere conducive to collaboration and empathy rather than competition and fear.

Understanding interpersonal dynamics is crucial; recognizing how different personalities interact can lead to improved teamwork while minimizing potential conflicts that might escalate tensions further. By fostering connections among colleagues—through team-building exercises or casual coffee chats—you strengthen bonds while enhancing morale within the workplace culture overall.

Incorporating these techniques into your daily life provides practical methods for managing stress effectively while navigating high-pressure work environments successfully! Whether through mindfulness practices designed around intentional living; engaging regularly in physical activities promoting both health benefits alongside mood elevation; utilizing quick breathing exercises aimed at calming frayed nerves; or building supportive communities encouraging collaboration—the strategies discussed here serve as essential tools empowering anyone seeking greater resilience amidst adversity!

* * *

Prioritizing Tasks Under Pressure

When you find yourself submerged in deadlines, multiple projects, and the constant buzz of workplace demands, effective prioritization becomes your lifeline. Managing tasks under pressure requires a clear strategy, enabling you to focus on what truly matters and navigate the chaos with confidence. Here's how you can master the art of prioritizing effectively, ensuring you stay productive even in the most challenging environments.

Assessing Impact and Urgency

The first step in prioritizing tasks is to evaluate their impact and urgency. Not all tasks hold equal weight; some have the potential to drive significant results while others may only occupy time without offering much return.

Begin by identifying which tasks demand immediate attention based on their potential impact. Ask yourself questions like: What will happen if I complete this task today? How does it contribute to my goals or my team's objectives? Understanding these elements helps discern what truly requires your focus.

To simplify this process, consider using the Eisenhower Matrix—a powerful tool that divides tasks into four quadrants based on urgency and importance:

1. **Urgent and Important**: These tasks require immediate action. They often come with looming deadlines or are critical to your success.
2. **Important but Not Urgent**: These tasks are essential for long-term success but do not require immediate action. Plan time for these to prevent them from becoming urgent.

3. **Urgent but Not Important**: Tasks in this category might seem pressing but don't significantly contribute to your overall goals. Delegate these when possible.
4. **Neither Urgent Nor Important**: These tasks can be dropped or postponed entirely, as they don't align with your priorities.

By categorizing your tasks within this framework, you gain clarity on what demands your attention first—allowing you to allocate your energy effectively.

Understanding the distinction between urgency and importance also aids in making informed decisions. Often, we confuse busywork with productivity. Remember that being busy doesn't equate to being effective; prioritize those activities that align with your strategic objectives instead.

Breaking Down Large Tasks

When faced with large projects, it's easy to feel overwhelmed by the scope of work ahead. This pressure can lead to paralysis—an inability to start due to the enormity of what needs doing. To combat this, break down larger tasks into smaller, manageable parts.

Start by dissecting a project into its core components or milestones. For instance, if you're tasked with launching a new product, identify individual steps such as market research, design development, testing phases, and marketing strategies.

Dividing larger tasks makes progress feel attainable because it allows you to focus on one step at a time rather than getting lost in the bigger picture. Each small win becomes a motivational boost under challenging conditions; celebrate these milestones as they signify movement toward completion.

Moreover, smaller milestones clarify the path forward. They provide structure amid chaos—offering specific targets that make it easier to allocate resources and manage time effectively. By achieving these mini-goals along the way, you not only build momentum but also reinforce a sense of accomplishment that counters feelings of overwhelm.

Establishing a Focused To-Do List

Creating a streamlined to-do list enhances focus and directs attention toward essential tasks—keeping distractions at bay even when pressure mounts.

Start by compiling a list of everything you need to accomplish within a specified timeframe—daily or weekly works best for maintaining relevance. However, don't let this list spiral out of control; aim for clarity and conciseness instead.

As you craft your list, prioritize it based on previously discussed criteria: identify which items are both urgent and important while eliminating less critical tasks that may detract from your primary goals. A focused list allows you to concentrate efforts where they matter most rather than spreading yourself thin across too many fronts.

Encourage daily or weekly revisions of this list to ensure alignment with current goals as situations change—new responsibilities might emerge unexpectedly while others lose significance over time. Regularly assessing priorities fosters adaptability without losing sight of progress made thus far.

Reassessing Priorities

Priorities aren't static—they evolve as circumstances shift around us. Therefore, regular reassessment ensures relevancy amid changing demands.

Make it a habit to take stock of ongoing projects weekly or bi-weekly;

check-in moments provide opportunities for course correction before minor issues escalate into major crises. Ask yourself whether existing priorities still serve your overarching objectives or if adjustments are needed based on newly emerging information.

This practice empowers you—not only does it prevent stagnation during periods of high pressure but also cultivates resilience in dynamic workplaces where rapid change is often the norm.

Gain insight into how priorities can fluctuate throughout different phases within projects; understanding that flexibility leads ultimately toward success can ease anxiety around uncertainty while building confidence over time as well!

* * *

Learning from Failure

Failure often gets a bad rap. We dread it, we avoid it, and we often see it as a reflection of our inadequacies. But what if we could flip that narrative? What if failure served as a stepping stone rather than a stumbling block? Shifting our perception of failure can pave the way for profound personal and professional growth.

Redefining Failure

To start, we must redefine failure. Instead of viewing it as a dead end, consider it an opportunity for growth. When you encounter setbacks, remind yourself that these moments are ripe with lessons waiting to be uncovered.

Think about your last misstep at work—maybe you missed an important deadline or failed to communicate effectively during a presentation. At first glance, those moments sting, but they also offer invaluable insights into what went wrong and how to improve next time. Viewing failures through this lens can transform them into powerful learning experiences that fuel future success.

Recognizing that setbacks are natural in any career journey fosters resilience. Everyone faces challenges—it's part of the game. Embracing this reality helps you bounce back stronger when the going gets tough. Acknowledging that failures are merely bumps on the road rather than signs of defeat cultivates a growth mindset, which is essential for continuous improvement.

Analyzing Mistakes

Now that we've reframed our understanding of failure, let's delve into how to analyze mistakes effectively. Reflective analysis is key to bolstering future success.

After experiencing a setback, take the time to conduct a thorough analysis of what happened. What went wrong? Were there external factors at play, or did you miss crucial steps in your process? Identifying patterns in your errors allows you to pinpoint areas needing improvement.

Reflection not only promotes accountability but also enhances problem-solving skills. By examining your missteps closely, you can uncover valuable strategies for overcoming similar challenges in the future. Documenting the lessons learned solidifies these experiences and provides a reference point for navigating new situations.

For instance, consider keeping a failure journal where you jot down specific instances of setbacks alongside reflections on what you learned from each experience. This practice encourages deeper self-awareness and creates a roadmap for avoiding similar pitfalls down the line.

Sharing Failures

While analyzing failures is crucial, sharing them with others can amplify their benefits exponentially. Open discussions about setbacks create a culture of trust and mutual growth within teams.

When team members feel comfortable sharing their failures without fear of judgment, everyone stands to gain valuable insights from each other's experiences. Learning from others' mistakes can expedite your personal development by offering new perspectives and solutions to common challenges.

Moreover, open dialogue about failure reduces the stigma around making mistakes and encourages vulnerability among colleagues. This shift in culture fosters stronger relationships built on empathy and understanding—essential elements for collaboration in any professional environment.

Imagine sitting around a conference table where team members openly share stories about projects that didn't go as planned and discuss what they learned from those experiences. This practice not only normalizes failure but also empowers individuals to approach their own challenges with newfound confidence.

Setting Future Goals Based on Insights

Finally, let's explore how to leverage insights gained from failures when setting future goals.

Using lessons learned from past missteps allows you to create actionable goals that help navigate similar situations moving forward. For example, if you recognize that poor communication led to misunderstandings during a project rollout, set specific goals aimed at improving your communication skills—whether through workshops or practicing active listening techniques with your team.

CHAPTER 4: THRIVING UNDER PRESSURE

Setting realistic goals informed by previous experiences fosters confidence in your ability to handle future challenges more effectively. This proactive approach emphasizes preparation over reaction; instead of waiting for another setback before addressing potential weaknesses, you actively seek ways to improve before issues arise.

This practice not only enhances individual performance but also contributes positively to team dynamics as well—when one person grows from their experiences, it raises the bar for everyone involved.

As we explore all these ideas together on learning from failure, keep in mind that every setback holds immense potential for growth if approached constructively. Failure isn't just something we should avoid; it's an integral part of career development—a stepping stone toward achieving greater heights in both personal and professional realms.

Chapter 5: Navigating Discrimination and Bias

As I sat at my desk, the hum of conversations floated around me. I couldn't help but notice how different my experience felt compared to some of my colleagues. Navigating the workplace often felt like walking a tightrope, balancing on the expectations set by others while managing the weight of biases that lingered in the air. Discrimination—whether based on gender, race, or age—often reared its head in subtle yet impactful ways.

This chapter aims to shine a light on those biases and provide you with tools to confront them head-on. We'll begin by recognizing unconscious biases that may not even register at first glance but shape our interactions every day. Then we'll dive into effective strategies for communicating assertively against discrimination when it occurs. Building allyship and support systems will also play a crucial role in fostering a more inclusive environment, reminding us that we don't have to navigate these challenges alone. Finally, I'll discuss the importance of documenting and reporting incidents to ensure accountability and change.

By the end of this chapter, you'll be equipped with insights and strategies to tackle discrimination and bias confidently in your own professional journey.

CHAPTER 5: NAVIGATING DISCRIMINATION AND BIAS

* * *

Recognizing Unconscious Biases

Let's dive into a critical yet often overlooked topic in our professional lives: unconscious biases. These are the biases we all hold, usually without realizing it, and they can significantly influence our interactions and decision-making in the workplace. By understanding these biases, we lay the groundwork for a more inclusive environment, allowing everyone to thrive.

What is Unconscious Bias?

Unconscious bias refers to the social stereotypes regarding specific groups of individuals that people form without conscious awareness. These biases affect how we think, feel, and behave towards others. You might not even realize it when you make a snap judgment about someone based on their gender, race, age, or any number of other characteristics.

In professional settings, these biases can manifest in various ways—during hiring processes, performance evaluations, team dynamics, or even everyday conversations. For instance, a hiring manager might unconsciously favor candidates who share similar backgrounds or experiences to their own. This bias not only impacts individual careers but also contributes to broader systemic inequalities.

Recognizing that unconscious bias exists is crucial for fostering an inclusive workplace. It serves as the first step toward mitigating its effects. When we begin to identify our own biases and those present in our organizations, we can take meaningful actions to counter them.

Common Types of Bias

Now that we have a foundational understanding of what unconscious bias is let's explore some common types:

By being aware of these specific biases within ourselves and others, we start identifying them in our daily interactions. This knowledge not only helps us cultivate empathy but also reduces the likelihood of engaging in prejudiced actions.

Impact of Bias on Self-Perception

It's important to understand how these unconscious biases shape our personal and professional identities. For example, if you're a woman working in a male-dominated industry and often find your contributions overlooked or dismissed due to gender bias, it can seriously undermine your confidence levels over time. You may start questioning your abilities or feeling inadequate compared to your male counterparts—regardless of your qualifications or experience.

Awareness of these dynamics allows us to confront the negative effects of bias head-on rather than internalizing them as truths about ourselves. When we understand that these biases exist within systems rather than as reflections of our worthiness or capabilities, it empowers us to take proactive steps toward personal empowerment.

Strategies for Self-Reflection

To effectively evaluate your own unconscious biases—and understand their implications—consider adopting some self-reflection techniques:

1. **Journaling**: Keeping a journal can help you articulate thoughts and feelings around situations where you suspect bias might

CHAPTER 5: NAVIGATING DISCRIMINATION AND BIAS

have influenced your judgments or behaviors. Reflecting on past interactions can uncover patterns that may need addressing.
2. **Seeking Feedback**: Engage with colleagues who may offer perspectives different from your own regarding potential blind spots in your behavior or decision-making processes. Honest feedback can serve as a mirror reflecting areas for improvement.
3. **Diverse Perspectives**: Make an effort to expose yourself to different viewpoints through reading diverse literature or engaging with varied communities online or offline. The more you immerse yourself in different experiences and stories, the more empathetic awareness you develop toward others' realities.

Regular self-assessment fosters personal growth by prompting behavioral changes and improving interactions with others—especially those who may come from different backgrounds than yours.

Recognizing one's own biases is key for effective allyship and support within any team dynamic or organizational structure. The journey toward confronting discrimination begins with each individual taking responsibility for their perspectives and behaviors—acknowledging that everyone has room for growth when it comes to understanding unconscious biases better.

Through these methods—defining what unconscious bias is, recognizing its common forms among ourselves and others, exploring its impact on self-perception, and implementing strategies for reflection—we build stronger foundations upon which inclusivity can flourish within our workplaces.

The road ahead may seem daunting at times; however, every small step taken toward awareness serves as progress—not just for oneself but for colleagues navigating similar challenges along the way.

* * *

Communicating Assertively Against Discrimination

Navigating the complex landscape of discrimination in the workplace requires more than just awareness; it demands a proactive approach to communication. When faced with unfair treatment or biases, how you express your concerns can significantly influence the outcome of the conversation. The ability to communicate assertively not only empowers you but also fosters an environment conducive to open dialogue.

Assertiveness vs. Aggression

Understanding the distinction between assertive communication and aggressive behavior is crucial. Assertiveness involves expressing your thoughts and feelings clearly and respectfully, without resorting to hostility or belittling others. It's about standing up for yourself while also acknowledging the rights and feelings of those around you.

On the other hand, aggression often leads to confrontational exchanges that can escalate tensions. This might involve raising your voice, using hostile language, or attacking someone personally rather than addressing their behavior. While it's natural to feel angry when confronted with discrimination, reacting aggressively typically backfires, pushing people away rather than encouraging understanding.

Assertive communication helps convey your message without causing defensiveness in others. When you articulate your feelings respectfully, confidence naturally builds. It sends a clear signal that you recognize your worth and expect others to do the same.

CHAPTER 5: NAVIGATING DISCRIMINATION AND BIAS

Techniques for Assertive Communication

Here are practical methods to express concerns about discrimination confidently:

1. **Utilize "I" Statements**: Positioning your feelings through "I" statements clarifies that you are speaking from personal experience rather than placing blame. For example, instead of saying "You never listen to my ideas," try "I feel overlooked when my suggestions aren't acknowledged." This shift in language allows for a more constructive dialogue.
2. **Prepare Responses**: Anticipate potential discriminatory remarks or situations that may arise during conversations. By preparing thoughtful responses in advance, you'll feel more equipped to address these challenges confidently when they occur.
3. **Role-Play Scenarios**: Practicing conversations through role-playing can significantly enhance your comfort level in real-life discussions. Gather a trusted friend or colleague and simulate various scenarios where you might encounter discrimination—this can help desensitize anxiety surrounding these discussions.

Managing Emotional Responses

Emotions can run high when discussing sensitive topics like discrimination; however, managing these emotional responses is key to maintaining effective communication:

1. **Emotional Regulation**: Learning how to regulate emotions allows for clearer expression under pressure. Techniques such as mindfulness practices can help you stay grounded during difficult conversations.

2. **Breathing Techniques**: Simple breathing exercises can make a substantial difference in moments of heightened emotion. Inhale deeply through your nose, hold for a few seconds, then exhale slowly through your mouth—repeating this process several times before responding can bring clarity and calmness.
3. **Pause for Thought**: Taking a moment before responding gives you space to collect your thoughts and ensures that your reaction isn't purely emotional but rather considered and intentional.

Keeping discussions focused on specific behaviors rather than generalizing about individuals helps prevent misunderstandings and unnecessary escalation of tensions.

Creating Supportive Dialogues

Engaging in constructive conversations about discrimination requires intentional strategies:

1. **Establish Common Ground**: Start by identifying shared values or experiences with the person you're communicating with; this fosters cooperation and understanding right from the outset. For instance, expressing mutual goals related to teamwork or workplace harmony can create an opening for discussing concerns without conflict.
2. **Promote Dialogue**: Encourage open discussions rather than one-sided monologues where only one party speaks at length without feedback from the other side. Promoting dialogue invites collective problem-solving; ask questions like "How do you see this situation?" or "What are some ways we could improve communication moving forward?" This approach helps diffuse potential defensiveness and opens pathways toward solutions.

3. **Active Listening**: To strengthen the communication process further, practice active listening techniques during these dialogues—this means truly hearing what others say instead of merely waiting for your turn to respond. Reflect back what you've heard by summarizing their points or asking clarifying questions like "So what I'm hearing is..." This not only validates their perspective but encourages them to reciprocate the same attentiveness when it's your turn to speak.

By fostering an atmosphere of respect and understanding through assertive communication techniques, you're not just addressing instances of discrimination; you're paving the way for more inclusive interactions moving forward.

As professionals navigating today's diverse workplaces, it's imperative we equip ourselves with tools that enable us not only to express our experiences but also encourage collective action against discrimination—all while maintaining our dignity and composure throughout each exchange we encounter along our career journeys.

* * *

Building Allyship and Support Systems

Allyship stands as a crucial pillar in the fight against discrimination, particularly in the workplace. When we define allyship, we see it as an active, consistent effort to support individuals from marginalized groups. Allies play a pivotal role by amplifying voices that often go unheard, advocating for equity, and helping to dismantle stigmas associated with discrimination.

Allies do more than just provide surface-level support; they cultivate a culture of inclusivity. By recognizing their privilege and using it to uplift others, they contribute to an environment where everyone feels valued and respected. Active allyship not only enhances individual confidence but also builds a more resilient professional atmosphere—one that can withstand the challenges of bias and inequity.

Understanding Allyship

The importance of allyship in the workplace cannot be overstated. It goes beyond mere friendship or camaraderie; it is about commitment and accountability. When allies actively work to understand the experiences of their colleagues from different backgrounds, they foster an environment where open dialogue thrives. This understanding allows for a greater appreciation of diverse perspectives, leading to innovative solutions that benefit everyone.

Moreover, allyship encourages collective resilience. When individuals know they have allies in their corner—people who are willing to stand up alongside them—they feel emboldened to confront discrimination head-on. In this way, allyship becomes not just an individual endeavor but a shared responsibility among all employees.

Finding Allies

Identifying and connecting with potential allies starts with intentional networking. Networking is not just about expanding your professional circle; it's about forging meaningful relationships based on mutual respect and shared values.

To begin finding allies within your organization:

1. **Identify Shared Values**: Look for colleagues who align with your beliefs regarding equity and inclusion. This might mean seeking

out individuals who have demonstrated support for marginalized voices or those who engage in discussions around social justice issues.
2. **Create Spaces for Open Dialogue**: Establish environments—be it during team meetings or informal gatherings—where open conversation can flourish. Invite colleagues to share their thoughts on diversity initiatives or experiences related to discrimination. By creating these spaces, you naturally invite potential allies into the conversation.
3. **Attend Workshops and Training**: Participating in workshops focused on diversity can connect you with like-minded individuals committed to fostering an inclusive workplace. These shared experiences provide a solid foundation for building supportive relationships.

By focusing on intentional networking, you lay the groundwork for creating alliances that not only empower you but also enrich the workplace culture as a whole.

Creating Support Networks

Once you've identified potential allies, the next step is forming support networks that provide each other with strength during challenging times. These networks serve as safe havens where individuals can share their experiences without fear of judgment.

Support groups offer several benefits:

1. **Safe Spaces for Sharing**: Within these groups, members can candidly discuss incidents of discrimination they've faced or witnessed. Sharing stories fosters understanding and creates solidarity among participants.

2. **Collaborative Problem Solving**: Diverse teams encourage varied perspectives when tackling issues related to discrimination or bias within the workplace. By collaborating with peers from different backgrounds, members enhance their problem-solving skills while developing empathy towards others' challenges.
3. **Peer Support Fosters Resilience**: Engaging with supportive colleagues helps cultivate resilience against external pressures stemming from discrimination. These networks not only motivate individuals but also encourage accountability—members hold one another responsible for fostering inclusivity within the broader organization.

By actively participating in support networks, employees create communities that enhance both individual well-being and collective strength.

Advocacy and Action

Building allyship involves taking concrete actions that empower everyone affected by discrimination. Advocacy initiatives can take many forms:

1. **Empowering Individuals**: Allies should actively speak out against injustice when they see it happening within their organizations. This may involve addressing discriminatory comments made during meetings or supporting colleagues facing unfair treatment from management.
2. **Collective Voice Influences Practices**: Organizing as a united front allows employees to collectively address policies that perpetuate inequities within their workplaces. A strong coalition of voices advocating for change significantly increases pressure on

CHAPTER 5: NAVIGATING DISCRIMINATION AND BIAS

leadership to reassess practices related to hiring, promotions, and organizational culture.
3. **Organizing Training Sessions**: Implementing training sessions focused on diversity and inclusion creates awareness among employees about systemic biases affecting marginalized groups within the organization; such training sessions cultivate empathy while informing employees how best they can support one another effectively.

By incorporating advocacy into everyday interactions at work—whether through speaking up against biases or promoting education around diversity—you help build stronger systems of allyship that stand ready to combat discrimination collaboratively.

In essence, forming strong support systems anchored by active allyship creates environments where all individuals feel empowered enough not only to thrive professionally but also personally amidst challenges stemming from inequality in today's diverse workplaces—a vital pursuit worth engaging wholeheartedly!

* * *

Documenting and Reporting Incidents

When faced with discrimination in the workplace, one of the most powerful tools at your disposal is documentation. Keeping detailed records not only serves as evidence for any formal complaints but also promotes a sense of empowerment. In this chapter, I'll guide you through effective documentation and reporting strategies to help protect yourself and others while navigating difficult situations.

Importance of Documentation

Documentation is crucial for several reasons. First, it serves as concrete evidence supporting claims made in formal complaints. When incidents occur, they can often feel overwhelming or confusing. Having a detailed record allows you to refer back to specific events, making it easier to articulate your experience when discussing the issue with HR or management.

Accurate records also strengthen your case when escalation becomes necessary. If you decide to take your complaint further—whether it's to upper management or even legal avenues—having well-documented incidents provides a clearer picture of what transpired. The more information you have, the better positioned you are to advocate for yourself.

Moreover, keeping a record of incidents promotes self-reflection on your experiences. Writing things down can help you process what happened, allowing for a deeper understanding of how these events affect your emotional well-being and professional life. This practice encourages personal growth while also serving as an important tool for accountability.

Best Practices for Documenting

Now that we've established why documentation is essential, let's discuss best practices for accurately documenting incidents of bias or discrimination:

1. **Capture Details**: Each entry should include specifics such as the date, time, location, and individuals who witnessed the incident. For instance:

CHAPTER 5: NAVIGATING DISCRIMINATION AND BIAS

- Date: March 15, 2023
- Time: 2:30 PM
- Location: Conference Room B
- Witnesses: John Smith, Emily Chen

Including these details not only adds credibility but also provides context that can be crucial later on.

1. **Be Objective**: Strive to keep your documentation as factual as possible. Avoid subjective language or emotional responses; instead, focus on what occurred without embellishment or personal interpretation. For example:

- Instead of writing "My manager was rude," document it as "During the team meeting, my manager interrupted me multiple times while I was speaking."

1. **Regular Updates**: Maintain an ongoing record by updating your documentation regularly. Whenever an incident occurs—no matter how minor it may seem—write it down promptly while details are fresh in your mind. This habit ensures that nothing slips through the cracks and creates a comprehensive account over time.
2. **Use Clear Language**: Write clearly and concisely so that anyone reading your documentation can easily understand what transpired without needing additional clarification.
3. **Keep Copies**: Store copies of all written documentation in a safe place where they can be easily accessed if needed later on.

By adhering to these best practices, you not only bolster your own confidence in handling discrimination but also equip yourself with essential tools should you need to escalate the matter further.

Reporting Mechanisms

Navigating workplace reporting procedures can often feel daunting; however, understanding company policies regarding discrimination reporting is vital for effective resolution:

1. **Familiarize Yourself with Company Policies**: Most organizations have established guidelines outlining how employees should report incidents of discrimination or bias. Take time to read through these policies thoroughly so that you know what steps are expected from you.
2. **Know Your Contacts**: Identify the appropriate contacts within your organization responsible for handling discrimination claims—this might include HR representatives or designated diversity officers. Knowing who to approach improves response times and ensures that your complaint reaches the right people.
3. **Utilize Established Channels**: When reporting incidents through official channels, ensure that you follow the protocol outlined by your company's policies closely—this could mean submitting written complaints via email or filling out specific forms provided by HR.
4. **Document Your Reports**: After submitting any formal report regarding discrimination claims, keep a copy for yourself along with notes about whom you spoke with and when any follow-up actions were promised.

Reporting incidents through established channels not only promotes accountability but also ensures that your organization takes appropriate action in response to concerns raised by employees.

CHAPTER 5: NAVIGATING DISCRIMINATION AND BIAS

Protecting Yourself from Retaliation

While reporting discrimination is vital for fostering change within organizations, it's equally important to ensure personal safety throughout this process:

1. **Know Your Rights**: Familiarize yourself with legal protections against retaliation for reporting discrimination; these laws exist precisely because individuals should feel secure when speaking up about wrongdoing without fear of negative repercussions.
2. **Seek External Support**: Consider reaching out to external organizations dedicated to protecting employee rights—such groups can provide guidance on navigating workplace issues while offering additional safeguarding measures during potentially challenging situations.
3. **Build a Support Network**: Cultivating relationships within your workplace can offer reassurance throughout this process; allies who understand what you're facing can provide encouragement when confronting adversity becomes overwhelming.

By proactively taking steps toward protection against retaliation while navigating reporting procedures successfully empowers both individuals experiencing discrimination and their allies working toward equitable environments together!

This commitment doesn't just benefit those directly involved—it contributes significantly towards fostering workplaces characterized by inclusivity where everyone has an opportunity thrive free from fear!

Chapter 6: Boosting Self-Esteem

As my career evolved, I often found myself trapped in a cycle of self-doubt. It wasn't just the high-pressure projects or demanding deadlines; it was the nagging voice in my head that told me I wasn't good enough. This internal dialogue became a barrier, hindering my ability to take risks and pursue opportunities that could elevate my professional journey. Over time, I learned that boosting self-esteem was not just a personal luxury but an essential component of success in any field.

In this chapter, we will explore several strategies designed to enhance self-esteem and foster a positive self-concept—tools that can transform how you perceive yourself and your capabilities.

First, we'll delve into **practicing self-compassion.** This approach encourages us to treat ourselves with the same kindness and understanding we would offer a friend facing similar struggles. By learning to embrace our imperfections rather than criticize them, we open the door to growth and resilience.

Next, we'll focus on **reinforcing positive affirmations.** These powerful statements serve as reminders of our worth and abilities. Crafting personalized affirmations can shift our mindset from one of doubt to one of empowerment. When we regularly repeat affirmations that resonate with us, they become embedded in our subconscious, gradually reshaping our self-image.

CHAPTER 6: BOOSTING SELF-ESTEEM

We'll also tackle the crucial task of *eliminating self-critical thoughts*. Many of us have perfected the art of negative self-talk—an unrelenting inner critic that undermines our confidence at every turn. By recognizing these destructive patterns and replacing them with constructive perspectives, we can create a healthier internal dialogue that supports our aspirations instead of sabotaging them.

Finally, we'll discuss the importance of *celebrating progress and successes*—no matter how small they may seem. Acknowledging achievements fosters a sense of accomplishment and reinforces our belief in our abilities. Whether it's completing a project on time or successfully navigating a challenging conversation, each victory deserves recognition.

Through these strategies, you'll not only boost your self-esteem but also cultivate an enduring sense of self-worth that empowers you in both personal and professional spheres. Let's dive deeper into these topics and discover how you can start this transformative journey today.

* * *

Practicing Self-Compassion

Self-compassion forms a vital part of our emotional toolkit, especially when navigating the tumultuous waters of professional life. At its core, self-compassion involves treating ourselves with the same kindness and understanding that we would offer to a friend facing hardship. When failure strikes or challenges arise, it's easy to fall into the trap of self-criticism, which only serves to erode our self-esteem further. Instead, practicing self-compassion can lead to improved resilience and emotional well-being.

Understanding self-compassion starts with acknowledging that everyone struggles at some point. Life is not a straight path; it's filled with twists and turns, highs and lows. Recognizing this shared human experience can normalize our own feelings of inadequacy when we stumble. Remembering that others face similar hurdles can help ease the burden of isolation often associated with self-doubt.

Embracing our imperfections is an essential aspect of self-compassion. None of us are perfect; we all have flaws and make mistakes. Instead of viewing these imperfections as weaknesses, consider them as opportunities for growth. Accepting that you're human allows you to approach your setbacks with curiosity rather than judgment. This shift in perspective fosters resilience, enabling you to bounce back more quickly from disappointments.

Moreover, developing self-compassion has been shown to decrease anxiety and stress levels significantly. When we're kind to ourselves during tough times, we create a buffer against negative emotions. It's easier to manage life's pressures when you have an internal support system cheering you on instead of one that constantly criticizes you.

To cultivate self-compassion effectively, consider incorporating some practical exercises into your daily routine:

1. **Daily Journaling Prompts**: Start each day or end each evening by writing down your thoughts. Use prompts like "What did I learn from today?" or "What challenges did I face?" As you identify negative self-talk—those harsh criticisms running through your mind—challenge them by replacing them with positive affirmations: "I am doing my best," or "I am worthy of love and respect." Journaling provides a safe space for reflection and helps solidify kinder narratives about yourself.

2. **Guided Meditations**: Seek out guided meditations focused on self-acceptance and compassion. These practices often lead you

through visualizations where you can cultivate feelings of warmth toward yourself. Set aside ten minutes daily to immerse yourself in these meditative experiences; they enhance your sense of worthiness and reinforce the idea that it's okay to be imperfect.
3. **Practicing Mindfulness**: Mindfulness plays a crucial role in staying grounded in the present moment while allowing feelings of compassion to surface naturally. By paying attention to your thoughts without judgment—acknowledging them and letting them pass—you can create space for compassion to grow in your heart rather than being overwhelmed by negativity.

While embracing self-compassion, it's also important to be aware of perfectionism—the relentless pursuit of flawlessness can hinder your journey toward higher self-esteem. Perfectionism breeds fear; it leads us to believe that unless we achieve our lofty standards, we are failures unworthy of respect or love.

Recognizing that perfection is unattainable can significantly reduce the pressure we place on ourselves and diminish the fear associated with potential failure. Instead of fixating solely on outcomes, shift your focus toward effort and growth. Acknowledge the work you've put in rather than obsessing over whether the result meets every idealized expectation.

Furthermore, understanding mistakes as valuable learning opportunities can transform how you view setbacks in both personal and professional contexts. When things don't go as planned, take time to analyze what went wrong—not through a lens of blame but as a constructive exercise aimed at growth.

Creating a supportive environment is also vital for nurturing self-compassion within yourself:

1. Surround yourself with positive influences—friends who uplift

rather than criticize can bolster your confidence immensely. Engaging with individuals who practice kindness themselves encourages you to adopt similar behaviors towards yourself.
2. Participate in groups focusing on self-compassion or personal development; such communities foster feelings of belonging while promoting healthier mindsets about success and failure.
3. Learn how to seek feedback from constructive sources; this means finding mentors or colleagues who offer insights designed for growth rather than criticism meant to tear down confidence levels.

As we continue this journey towards enhanced self-esteem through practicing self-compassion, remember that being kind to yourself isn't just an act—it's a commitment towards nurturing your emotional well-being every day.

Incorporating these practices into your life might take time, but the investment will pay dividends in how you perceive yourself amid challenges ahead—an invaluable asset on any professional path!

* * *

Reinforcing Positive Affirmations

Imagine waking up in the morning, the sun just peeking through your curtains, and instead of scrolling through your phone or diving into a to-do list, you take a moment for yourself. You stand in front of the mirror, look yourself in the eye, and recite a few affirmations that resonate with you. This simple act can set a powerful tone for your day and has the potential to transform how you perceive yourself and your capabilities.

Creating personal affirmations is about crafting meaningful statements that reflect your aspirations, strengths, and values. Start by thinking about what you want to reinforce in your life. Are there specific areas where you struggle? Perhaps self-doubt creeps in when you face new challenges at work or during social interactions. Write down phrases that counter those doubts.

For example, if you often think, "I'm not good enough," turn that negative belief on its head: "I am capable and worthy of success." The key is relevance; affirmations must speak to you personally to have any real impact.

In celebrating your uniqueness, consider how these affirmations reflect who you are. You might say something like, "I embrace my individuality; my perspective is valuable." This kind of statement acknowledges that you are not only different but that those differences contribute positively to the world around you.

The repetition of affirmations is crucial in reinforcing positive beliefs about oneself. The more frequently you repeat an affirmation, the more likely it becomes embedded in your subconscious mind. As with any skill, practice is essential. Repeating affirmations helps form neural pathways associated with self-acceptance and positivity.

Now, let's talk about integrating these affirmations into your daily routine. Creating a morning ritual that includes affirmations can set a positive tone for the day ahead. As soon as you wake up—before getting caught up in work emails or social media—take five minutes to stand before a mirror and recite your chosen affirmations. This practice helps prime your mind for positivity and resilience.

Additionally, connecting affirmations to specific triggers can enhance consistency in practice. Consider placing visual reminders around your home or workspace—sticky notes on your bathroom mirror or computer monitor with key phrases like "I am enough" or "I attract opportunities." These reminders serve as nudges throughout the day, encouraging a mindset shift whenever negativity arises.

Practicing affirmations in front of a mirror builds confidence through self-acknowledgment. When I stand there looking at myself while confidently stating my worth or abilities, it's as though I'm having an empowering conversation with my reflection. It may feel strange at first; perhaps even uncomfortable—but this discomfort dissipates over time as self-love grows stronger.

However, we all encounter negative self-talk from time to time—those insidious thoughts that creep into our minds uninvited. To counteract this negativity effectively requires intention and strategy. Begin by identifying personal negative beliefs: What do you find yourself telling yourself? Is it something like "I always mess things up"? Once recognized, address these beliefs head-on with counter-affirmations: "Mistakes are opportunities for growth."

Transforming criticism into actionable affirmations fosters growth rather than discouragement. For instance, if someone criticizes your work performance and it stings deeply, instead of internalizing their judgment as proof of inadequacy, remind yourself: "I learn from feedback; it makes me stronger." This approach not only softens the blow but also reinforces resilience.

Developing awareness of recurring negative thoughts empowers proactive change as well. Keep track of moments when self-doubt arises or when criticism gets under your skin; this reflection will help build insight into triggers so they can be addressed more consciously with corresponding positive statements moving forward.

Sharing affirmations with others can amplify their power even further—think about engaging within supportive communities where individuals exchange affirmations regularly! Being part of such groups enhances motivation while fostering accountability among members who uplift one another through shared positivity.

Imagine being surrounded by peers who encourage each other to declare daily goals or aspirations aloud—a culture of collective empowerment takes shape! Recognizing the impact this has on individual resolve creates an environment conducive not just for personal growth but community bonding too.

When we inspire others through shared experiences—whether it's giving compliments or exchanging uplifting messages—we cultivate a ripple effect; our words resonate beyond ourselves! Engaging with like-minded individuals allows affirmation practices not only to benefit us personally but extend support towards creating empowered atmospheres filled with encouragement.

Incorporating positive affirmations into daily life isn't merely an exercise in feel-good rhetoric—it's about actively reshaping how we view ourselves and respond to challenges along our journeys together! Embracing positivity transforms our mindsets from scarcity-focused ones filled with doubt towards abundance-driven ones brimming with potential!

By reinforcing these principles daily through intentional practices rooted within authenticity while leaning on communities for encouragement—we craft lives infused with confidence while boldly pursuing goals unencumbered by fear!

* * *

Eliminating Self-Critical Thoughts

Self-critical thoughts can sneak into our minds like uninvited guests, lingering and leaving us feeling inadequate. These internal dialogues often tell us we're not good enough, that we'll never succeed, or that our failures define who we are. Understanding how to identify and combat these destructive thoughts is crucial for building self-esteem and nurturing a supportive inner dialogue.

Recognizing Negative Thought Patterns

Awareness of destructive self-talk is the first step toward change. Many of us fall into patterns of negative thinking without even realizing it. Statements like "I'm not smart enough," or "I always mess things up" are common culprits. These phrases serve as a backdrop to our daily lives, quietly chipping away at our confidence.

One effective technique is to keep a journal specifically dedicated to tracking your negative thoughts. Write down any self-critical remarks you catch yourself making throughout the day. This exercise will help clarify patterns and triggers associated with your negative thinking. You might notice that certain situations—like giving a presentation or meeting new people—trigger a barrage of critical thoughts. Recognizing these patterns allows you to prepare for them and develop strategies for overcoming them.

Once you've identified these destructive patterns, it's essential to challenge their validity. Ask yourself questions like: "Is this thought really true?" or "What evidence do I have to support this belief?" Promoting critical thinking about your own thoughts can help dismantle their power over you.

Reframing Negative Thoughts

Now that you're aware of your self-critical thoughts, it's time to shift gears and reframe them into constructive feedback. For example, instead of telling yourself, "I can't do this," try reframing it as, "I am capable of learning." This subtle change in language transforms a fixed mindset into one focused on growth.

To encourage further reframing, ask yourself empowering questions when you catch yourself in negative thought spirals. Questions like, "What would I tell a friend who feels this way?" or "How can I view this situation from a different perspective?" help you break free from rigid thinking patterns.

Adopting a growth mindset can diminish fear and self-doubt significantly. Embracing the belief that abilities can be developed through dedication and hard work fosters resilience in the face of challenges. Remind yourself that everyone encounters obstacles; what matters is how we respond to them.

Practicing Self-Forgiveness

Self-forgiveness is vital for emotional healing and personal growth. Understanding that everyone makes mistakes encourages compassion towards oneself instead of wallowing in guilt or shame. When faced with failure or setbacks, recognize that it's part of being human—it doesn't define your worth.

One strategy for practicing self-forgiveness involves writing a letter to yourself as if you were addressing a friend who had experienced similar setbacks. Express empathy and understanding; remind yourself that mistakes are opportunities for learning rather than indicators of inadequacy.

Developing rituals for self-forgiveness can also promote emotional healing. Create moments where you consciously let go of past errors—this could be through meditation, visualization exercises, or affirmations focused on acceptance and growth. Engaging in activities that bring joy or relaxation can also serve as reminders to treat ourselves with kindness rather than harsh criticism.

Creating Positive Internal Dialogue

Cultivating a supportive internal narrative requires intentional effort but yields significant benefits over time. One practical approach is establishing a buddy system where individuals affirm each other's strengths and accomplishments regularly. Surrounding yourself with positive influences reinforces your commitment to nurturing a more compassionate inner voice.

Additionally, consider verbal agreements with yourself; set intentions for how you want to speak internally each day—"Today I will focus on my strengths" or "I will acknowledge my progress." These statements serve as anchors guiding your mindset toward positivity throughout the day.

Implementing regular self-reflection sessions helps identify progress made in combating self-critical thoughts over time too! Set aside time weekly to assess what went well during the week regarding positive affirmations practiced or instances where reframing occurred successfully. Reflecting on growth creates momentum toward further improvement while reminding ourselves just how far we've come!

* * *

Celebrating Progress and Successes

In the hustle and bustle of our daily lives, we often overlook one crucial element: celebrating our progress. We set goals, work tirelessly, and sometimes forget to acknowledge the small victories that pave the way to greater achievements. Recognizing and celebrating these milestones can significantly enhance our self-esteem and reinforce a positive self-concept.

Setting Milestones

To truly appreciate our journey, it's essential to break our goals into manageable milestones. These stepping stones serve as markers along the path toward success. Setting realistic milestones not only boosts motivation but also fosters self-confidence. When you achieve these smaller objectives, it feels like a victory—each success builds on the last.

Consider this: when I first started mentoring colleagues, I didn't jump into major projects right away. Instead, I set smaller milestones. My initial goal was to facilitate a single team meeting effectively. Once I accomplished that, I aimed to lead a workshop on effective communication skills. Each of these steps represented a significant achievement that propelled me forward.

Recognizing small achievements fosters a sense of accomplishment that keeps us motivated. It's vital to celebrate these moments because they remind us of our progress and capabilities. Additionally, re-evaluating and adjusting our goals as we move forward encourages sustained growth; we learn from each experience and can modify our path as needed.

Documenting Achievements

Another effective strategy for acknowledging progress is documenting your achievements. Keeping track of your successes provides a tangible reminder of how far you've come. A success journal, or private blog, can help visualize growth and reinforce self-worth. In this journal, jot down every achievement—no matter how small—alongside the date it occurred.

Frequent reflection on past accomplishments can provide inspiration during challenging times. When self-doubt creeps in, flipping through your success journal serves as a powerful reminder of your abilities and resilience.

Moreover, sharing accomplishments with trusted peers enhances feelings of validation. When you vocalize your successes, you invite others to celebrate with you—this communal acknowledgment strengthens bonds and fosters encouragement within your network.

Developing Celebration Rituals

Celebration rituals are another essential aspect of recognizing achievements meaningfully. Simple practices can amplify feelings of success significantly. For instance, treating yourself after reaching a milestone—whether that's enjoying your favorite dessert or taking time off for self-care—creates positive reinforcement for your hard work.

Consider creating communal celebrations with supportive colleagues too; organizing small gatherings or recognition events where everyone shares their wins cultivates connection among team members. These moments create an atmosphere of support that enhances motivation for everyone involved.

Reinforcing the idea that celebration is key to sustaining motivation cannot be overstated. By establishing routines for recognizing achievements—both big and small—you build an environment where success is celebrated regularly rather than just at significant milestones.

Learning from Every Experience

Finally, it's essential to view all experiences as valuable lessons along your journey toward confidence-building and professional development. Emphasizing gratitude for experiences—both positive and negative—nurtures resilience within ourselves.

CHAPTER 6: BOOSTING SELF-ESTEEM

Reflecting on what you've learned from both triumphs and setbacks helps strengthen future efforts; consider what went well during successful moments while also evaluating what could be improved when faced with challenges. This balanced perspective empowers personal growth by encouraging continuous learning rather than dwelling on perceived failures.

Building a culture of self-recognition contributes significantly to sustaining long-term confidence as well! When individuals recognize their worth through celebration regularly, they cultivate an internal dialogue that emphasizes positivity instead of criticism—a vital ingredient for ongoing success in any endeavor!

Chapter 7: The Power of Networking

In my journey through the corporate landscape, I quickly learned that the connections I forged often held more weight than the skills I had honed. Networking is more than just a buzzword; it's a lifeline for career advancement, a bridge to new opportunities, and a source of invaluable support. When I first began my career, I felt hesitant to engage with others. However, as I navigated the complexities of various roles—from recruiter to delivery director—I discovered that networking opened doors I never knew existed.

This chapter delves into the power of networking and how it can shape your professional path. First, we'll explore **Identifying Networking Opportunities**. Whether at industry conferences, local meetups, or even informal gatherings, recognizing where you can connect with like-minded individuals is crucial. These environments not only foster introductions but also provide fertile ground for exchanging ideas and insights.

Next up is **Cultivating Meaningful Relationships**. Building a network isn't merely about collecting business cards or LinkedIn connections; it's about nurturing relationships that can offer mutual support. In my experience, taking the time to get to know others on a personal level—sharing experiences, challenges, and triumphs—has led to stronger bonds that stand the test of time.

We'll then shift our focus to **Effectively Utilizing Social Media**.

CHAPTER 7: THE POWER OF NETWORKING

Platforms like LinkedIn have transformed networking from an in-person experience into a digital landscape where connections can flourish. I'll share strategies for leveraging these tools to enhance your visibility and engagement within your industry while showcasing your unique value.

Finally, we'll discuss **Understanding the Value of Mentorship**. Having mentors throughout my career has been instrumental in guiding me through challenges and helping me seize opportunities. This section will highlight how finding a mentor can provide you with insights that are often difficult to access otherwise and how you can become a mentor yourself.

As we navigate this chapter together, keep in mind that each connection has the potential to enrich your professional life in unexpected ways. Let's dive into how you can harness the power of networking for your own success.

* * *

Identifying Networking Opportunities

Networking isn't just a professional buzzword; it's a crucial component of career advancement and personal growth. As you navigate your career path, identifying networking opportunities can lead to valuable connections, collaborations, and insights that may transform your trajectory. Let's explore various avenues for networking that suit your professional landscape, emphasizing both formal and informal interactions.

Industry Events

One of the most effective ways to network is by attending industry events such as conferences, seminars, and trade shows. These gatherings draw together like-minded professionals eager to share knowledge and forge connections.

Imagine walking into a bustling conference hall filled with individuals who share your passion for technology or leadership. The energy in the room is palpable as people exchange ideas and experiences. This environment fosters valuable face-to-face interactions that can lead to meaningful connections. You might meet someone who works at a company you're interested in or an expert in your field who can offer insights you haven't considered.

Networking at these events opens doors for potential job opportunities or collaborations. For instance, I remember attending a tech conference where I met a project manager from a leading firm. Our conversation revealed mutual interests in Agile methodologies, and we exchanged contact information. A few weeks later, she reached out about an open position on her team—one I wouldn't have known about had we not connected at that event.

Additionally, engaging in discussions at these gatherings enhances your industry knowledge. Participating in panel discussions or workshops provides not only the chance to learn but also the opportunity to contribute your thoughts and expertise. This proactive approach positions you as an engaged participant rather than just an observer.

Professional Organizations

Joining relevant industry groups or associations expands your network significantly. Professional organizations often provide access to exclusive resources and connections that can be instrumental for career development. Membership in these organizations typically includes invitations to networking events, professional development workshops, and conferences tailored to your industry. For example, being part of an organization dedicated to women in technology can connect you with influential leaders who understand the unique challenges you may face.

Engaging actively within these organizations can lead to mentorship relationships that are crucial for growth. Mentors often have valuable experience and insights that can help guide you through challenges or decisions you face in your career journey. They might also introduce you to other professionals within their network, further expanding your connections.

Moreover, many organizations have online forums or discussion boards where members can ask questions and share advice. Contributing to these conversations helps establish your presence within the community while providing learning opportunities from peers facing similar challenges.

Online Webinars and Panels

In today's digital age, online webinars and panels offer excellent opportunities for networking with professionals globally without geographical limitations. These virtual events allow for interaction with experts and industry leaders from diverse backgrounds right from the comfort of your home or office.

Participating in these platforms facilitates connections with individuals you might never meet otherwise—those who are across the country or even around the world. During webinars focused on specific topics of interest, engaging through Q&A sessions can put you on the radar of key players in your field.

For instance, consider attending a webinar led by a thought leader discussing trends in project management tools. By asking thoughtful questions during the session, not only do you enhance your understanding of the topic at hand, but you also create an opportunity for follow-up conversations afterward—whether through social media or email.

The relationships formed through online networking can lead to collaborations and partnerships that enrich your career journey. Connecting with someone who shares similar interests may result in joint projects or initiatives down the line.

Social Gatherings

Finally, don't underestimate the power of informal events like meetups or social gatherings for networking purposes. While they may seem less structured than formal conferences or organizational meetings, informal settings often allow for more relaxed interactions that foster genuine relationships.

At casual gatherings such as happy hours or community meetups, people are usually more open and willing to share personal stories alongside their professional experiences. This creates an environment where deeper relationships can form organically—a refreshing change from the sometimes rigid structure of formal networking events.

These casual conversations may yield unexpected insights or referrals that might not surface in traditional settings. For example, during a local meetup focused on entrepreneurship, I struck up a conversation with another attendee about our experiences launching startups. Our exchange revealed we faced similar hurdles; we ended up exchanging contacts—and later collaborated on a project leveraging each other's strengths.

Engaging informally allows for connection on a personal level; after all, people do business with those they know and trust. By nurturing these authentic relationships over time—through coffee catch-ups or social media exchanges—you lay a strong foundation that supports both personal growth and professional opportunities.

In conclusion, identifying various networking opportunities—from industry events and professional organizations to online webinars and informal gatherings—can significantly impact your career trajectory. By actively seeking out these avenues for connection and engagement within your professional landscape, you open doors not only for job prospects but also for collaboration and mentorship that could propel you toward greater success.

* * *

Cultivating Meaningful Relationships

Building meaningful professional relationships is essential for both personal and career growth. These connections provide a support system that can lead to fruitful collaborations, new opportunities, and a sense of belonging in your field. Let's explore effective strategies to cultivate these relationships.

Follow-Up Strategies

After meeting someone new—whether at a networking event or through an introduction—follow-up is crucial. Staying in touch demonstrates your genuine interest and commitment to nurturing the relationship. It's easy to let initial interactions fade into memory, but with a little effort, you can keep those connections alive.

Consider sending a brief email or message within a few days of your meeting. Reference something specific from your conversation to show that you were engaged. A simple line like, "I really enjoyed our chat about your approaches to conducting customer surveys and how they simplify making software products much more usable," can go a long way in reinforcing the connection.

Regular communication keeps you top of mind when opportunities arise within their networks. You never know when someone might be looking for recommendations or collaborators; being proactive can place you at the forefront of their thoughts.

Personalizing your messages can deepen connections significantly. Instead of generic follow-ups, mention articles or events that may interest them based on your discussions. For instance, if they mentioned an interest in leadership strategies, sharing a relevant book or article you found could spark further dialogue.

Reciprocal Support

Reciprocity is the backbone of strong professional relationships. Offering assistance or resources in return for support received creates bonds that are both stronger and more sustainable. It's important to remember that relationships should not be one-sided; they thrive on mutual give-and-take.

When someone provides help—whether it's advice on a project or an introduction to another contact—consider how you can reciprocate. This doesn't always mean returning the favor immediately; sometimes it involves being proactive in offering assistance down the line.

Collaborating on projects also enhances mutual respect and understanding. When you work together towards shared goals, you develop insights into each other's strengths and weaknesses, fostering deeper connections built on trust.

Additionally, sharing knowledge or resources strengthens goodwill among colleagues. If you come across valuable information that aligns with their interests or challenges they're facing, don't hesitate to share it without expecting anything in return. This generosity often results in increased goodwill and strengthens the foundation of your relationship.

Shared Interests and Goals

Finding common ground is crucial for reinforcing professional relationships. Identifying shared values or objectives creates a foundation for deeper discussions and enhances collaboration potential.

Engaging in projects together can solidify these bonds further. When you're aligned with someone on shared goals—whether it's improving team communication processes or launching a new initiative—the synergy often leads to successful outcomes.

Conversations about mutual interests frequently spark innovative ideas and collaborations as well. For example, if two professionals share an enthusiasm for environmental sustainability within their industries, brainstorming ways to implement greener practices could lead to impactful initiatives—and potentially lucrative partnerships down the road.

Consider hosting informal meetups centered around shared interests, such as book clubs focusing on leadership literature or workshops aimed at developing specific skills relevant to your field. These gatherings allow participants not only to bond over their passions but also facilitate collaborative learning experiences.

Networking Etiquette

Understanding and respecting boundaries in networking interactions is key to maintaining positive relationships. Politeness and respect build a favorable reputation within your network; people remember those who treat them well.

It's essential to recognize when to engage actively and when to step back; overzealousness can overwhelm contacts rather than strengthen ties. Gauge their responses during conversations—if someone seems distracted or disinterested, it may be time to pivot the discussion or give them space.

Practicing active listening shows dedication toward building rapport with others. Pay attention during conversations without letting distractions interfere; this indicates respect for what they have to say while enhancing connection quality overall.

By focusing on these aspects of cultivating meaningful relationships—following up thoughtfully, offering reciprocal support, identifying shared interests, and practicing networking etiquette—you'll lay the groundwork for strong professional bonds that contribute positively throughout your career journey.

* * *

Effectively Utilizing Social Media

Navigating the ever-evolving landscape of social media can feel daunting, especially when it comes to leveraging these platforms for professional growth. However, with a clear strategy, you can harness social media to build your network, increase your visibility, and propel your career forward.

Choosing the Right Platforms

First things first: identifying which platforms align best with your professional goals is essential. Each social media site serves different purposes and caters to unique audiences.

LinkedIn stands out as the prime platform for professionals. It allows you to connect with colleagues, industry leaders, and potential employers while showcasing your skills and experiences. Regularly engaging with content on LinkedIn keeps you informed about industry trends and opens doors to networking opportunities. Consider following relevant companies or thought leaders in your field to enhance your feed with insightful information.

On the other hand, X (formerly Twitter) provides a dynamic space for real-time conversations. You can engage directly with thought leaders and participate in current discussions that matter in your industry. Use hashtags strategically to discover trending topics and join conversations that resonate with your professional interests.

Understanding where your industry congregates online helps maximize your networking efforts. Whether it's niche forums or dedicated Facebook groups, exploring various platforms broadens the horizons for potential connections.

Creating an Engaging Profile

Once you've chosen the right platforms, optimizing your profiles becomes crucial in attracting connections and opportunities. Your online presence is often the first impression you make on potential employers or collaborators.

A well-crafted profile highlights not just your skills but also your experiences and aspirations. Use a professional photo; it may seem trivial, but a friendly yet polished image can go a long way in making you approachable.

Beyond visuals, consider crafting an engaging summary that encapsulates who you are professionally. This summary should reflect not only what you've accomplished but also where you're headed—your ambitions matter too!

Engaging content—like articles or insights into industry trends—establishes credibility and attracts attention. Share thoughtful posts about projects you're working on or recent developments in your field; this signals that you're active and invested in continuous learning.

Don't forget about regular updates; keeping your profile fresh informs your network about your latest endeavors. Did you attend a workshop? Completed a certification? Share those milestones!

Engagement Strategies

After establishing an engaging profile, actively participating in discussions becomes vital for enhancing visibility within your network. Commenting on posts isn't just about adding noise; it's an opportunity to showcase knowledge while fostering relationships.

When you share relevant content from others or contribute thoughtful comments on discussions within groups or threads, you're increasing both your presence and goodwill within the community. These interactions can prompt reciprocation—when you engage with others' content, they are more likely to return the favor by engaging with yours.

Hosting online discussions or Q&A sessions can position you as a thought leader in your area of expertise. Consider organizing webinars or informal virtual meetups focused on topics of interest within your industry. These gatherings not only showcase what you know but also create spaces for connection among participants.

Furthermore, consider collaborating with peers on projects that leverage each other's strengths; such partnerships not only expand networks but foster deeper relationships based on mutual support.

Building a Diverse Network

Finally, seek out individuals from various backgrounds and industries when building connections online. A diverse network can provide fresh perspectives and varied opportunities that may not exist within traditional circles.

Encouraging connections beyond immediate fields leads to unexpected collaborations—consider reaching out to professionals from different sectors who may offer insights applicable to yours. For instance, someone from marketing could provide valuable strategies for communicating technical ideas more effectively; this type of cross-pollination enhances innovation across disciplines.

Moreover, being open to learning from different industries broadens skillsets and experiences significantly. Attend events outside of typical networking scenarios; join groups related to hobbies or interests unrelated to work—they often yield surprising opportunities!

By thoughtfully navigating social media—selecting suitable platforms, crafting compelling profiles, engaging meaningfully with others' content, and expanding networks—you'll unlock doors leading towards personal growth and professional advancement.

* * *

Understanding the Value of Mentorship

Mentorship plays a crucial role in professional growth and confidence building. Having someone who can guide you through the complexities of your career can be a game-changer. A mentor not only shares valuable insights but also helps you navigate challenges and make informed decisions that shape your path.

Finding a Mentor

Identifying the right mentor is the first step. Look within your organization or industry for individuals who have experience and knowledge relevant to your goals. This targeted approach ensures that you receive guidance tailored to your specific circumstances.

Networking events are excellent opportunities to meet potential mentors. Engage with speakers, panelists, or fellow attendees—these interactions can lead to fruitful connections. When you approach someone for mentorship, be clear about what you're seeking. Whether it's career advice, skill development, or industry insights, articulating your needs helps potential mentors understand how they can support you.

When reaching out, don't hesitate to share your aspirations and why you admire their work. A genuine compliment goes a long way in establishing rapport and making them more inclined to assist you.

Establishing a Mentorship Relationship

Once you've identified a potential mentor, cultivating that relationship requires effort. Setting regular meetings creates structure and accountability in your mentorship journey. During these sessions, discuss specific goals; having a clear focus helps both parties make the most of their time together.

Preparation is key—thoroughly preparing for each meeting demonstrates your commitment to the mentorship relationship. Arrive with questions, updates on progress, and reflections on previous discussions. This level of engagement not only shows respect for your mentor's time but also reinforces the collaborative nature of the relationship.

Feedback is vital too; sharing how their advice has impacted your journey keeps the lines of communication open and encourages deeper conversations about mutual growth.

Learning Opportunities

Mentors offer invaluable learning opportunities through their critiques and insights. They can help refine your skills by providing constructive feedback based on real-life experiences. Their stories about navigating challenges provide context that prepares you to handle similar situations when they arise.

For instance, if a mentor shares how they overcame setbacks in their career, it equips you with strategies to manage adversity effectively. Understanding their successes and failures can serve as powerful lessons—allowing you to adapt their approaches to fit your unique circumstances.

Additionally, mentoring relationships create safe spaces where candid discussions can occur without fear of judgment. This trust fosters open dialogue about aspirations and anxieties alike.

Giving Back

Mentorship isn't just about receiving guidance; it's also about giving back. Once you've gained insights and developed confidence through mentoring relationships, consider becoming a mentor yourself. This transition fosters personal growth while supporting others in their journeys.

Teaching others strengthens your own understanding of concepts as you explain them from different perspectives. It reinforces what you've learned while also expanding your professional network as you connect with new individuals seeking guidance.

Furthermore, mentorship creates a cycle of support within industries—a chain reaction that benefits future professionals just starting out on their paths. As more individuals take on mentoring roles, the community grows stronger through shared knowledge and experiences.

In summary, understanding the value of mentorship highlights its importance in building confidence and advancing careers. By finding the right mentors, establishing meaningful relationships, seizing learning opportunities from those experiences, and ultimately giving back as mentors ourselves—we contribute to an environment that fosters continuous growth for all involved.

Chapter 8: Resilience and Adaptability

In today's fast-paced work environment, resilience has become a vital skill. It's not just about weathering the storm; it's about learning to dance in the rain. I've learned that adaptability isn't merely a trait; it's a practice that I've had to cultivate throughout my career. When challenges arise, they often shake our foundations, but developing mental resilience allows us to bounce back stronger.

This chapter dives into essential strategies for building that resilience. First, we'll explore **Building Mental Resilience**—the process of fortifying our minds against stress and setbacks. Throughout my journey, I faced numerous hurdles that tested my resolve. Each experience taught me that resilience doesn't mean avoiding difficulties but confronting them head-on and learning from them.

Next, we'll shift our focus to **Embracing Change as an Opportunity**. Change is often uncomfortable; it disrupts our routines and can instill fear of the unknown. However, I've discovered that viewing change as a chance for growth opens up new avenues for success. This perspective has transformed how I approach both personal and professional transitions.

Then, we'll discuss **Developing Flexibility in Work Approaches**. In an era where remote work and agile methodologies have taken center stage, flexibility has become paramount. Adapting our methods and processes to meet the needs of evolving projects not only enhances productivity but also fosters innovation within teams. I learned to embrace varied approaches rather than cling tightly to what felt familiar.

Lastly, we'll address **Setting Boundaries to Avoid Burnout**. In my early years in the corporate world, I often pushed myself too hard—thinking it was a sign of dedication when it was really leading me down the path of exhaustion. Understanding the importance of setting boundaries helped me create a sustainable work-life balance that promotes long-term success.

As we navigate this chapter together, keep in mind that building resilience isn't a one-time effort; it's an ongoing journey of self-discovery and growth. Each section will equip you with actionable insights to help you thrive in any environment you encounter.

* * *

Building Mental Resilience

Mental resilience—the ability to bounce back from setbacks—is a cornerstone of personal and professional success. In the ever-changing landscape of the workplace, challenges and hurdles are inevitable. Understanding how to cultivate this resilience not only maintains confidence but also enables you to thrive under pressure.

Resilience is more than just enduring tough times; it's about growing from them. Those who build mental resilience can navigate stressful situations with greater ease and emerge stronger on the other side. This capacity significantly impacts career advancement and personal growth, allowing individuals to embrace opportunities rather than shy away from them.

To strengthen your mental fortitude, several practical techniques can be incorporated into daily work life.

Understanding Mental Resilience

At its core, mental resilience equips you with the tools needed to manage stress and recover from adversity. When faced with obstacles—be it a missed deadline or a difficult conversation—those with higher resilience are less likely to feel overwhelmed. They possess a mindset that allows them to view setbacks as temporary challenges rather than insurmountable barriers.

Building mental resilience starts with recognizing that setbacks are part of any journey. Accepting this reality lays the groundwork for developing coping strategies that enable effective responses in challenging situations.

Techniques to Build Resilience

Mindfulness is one technique that plays a vital role in enhancing resilience. By practicing mindfulness, you train yourself to focus on the present moment rather than getting lost in worries about the past or future. This heightened awareness fosters clarity during stressful times, allowing for more rational decision-making.

Cognitive restructuring is another powerful tool in your arsenal. This technique involves challenging negative thought patterns and replacing them with more constructive perspectives. For example, if you find yourself thinking, "I'll never get this project done," reframe it as, "I have faced difficult projects before and succeeded; I can break this down into manageable steps." Regular practice of cognitive restructuring shifts your perspective toward challenges, enabling you to see failures as opportunities for learning rather than signs of inadequacy.

Both mindfulness and cognitive restructuring contribute to emotional intelligence—your ability to recognize and manage your emotions as well as understand those of others. Higher emotional intelligence enhances conflict resolution skills and strengthens interpersonal relationships, which leads us to our next point: the importance of positive relationships in building resilience.

The Role of Positive Relationships

Surrounding yourself with supportive colleagues can be a game-changer when navigating workplace challenges. Strong professional relationships provide encouragement during tough times, reminding you that you're not alone in facing difficulties. When a colleague offers their perspective or simply listens while you vent frustrations, it reinforces your capacity for resilience.

Building a network of support fosters collaboration within the work environment. A culture where colleagues uplift one another creates an atmosphere where individuals feel safe sharing ideas and seeking help without fear of judgment. Positive interactions reinforce resilience by offering diverse viewpoints on challenges, making them seem less daunting when approached collectively.

Consider a team project where tensions ran high due to conflicting opinions among members. One team member stepped up and organized regular check-ins—an opportunity for everyone to voice concerns while focusing on solutions rather than problems. These meetings strengthened connections among team members, enabling them all to tackle the project together with renewed vigor.

CHAPTER 8: RESILIENCE AND ADAPTABILITY

Real-Life Examples

Looking at other people brings an understanding that resilience is attainable for everyone. Take my friend Sarah—a marketing manager who faced significant pressure during her company's rebranding initiative. As deadlines loomed closer, her initial enthusiasm began wavering under the weight of expectations.

Instead of succumbing to stress, Sarah decided to employ mindfulness techniques during her breaks at work. By taking five minutes each hour for focused breathing exercises or short walks outside, she recalibrated her mind before diving back into her tasks. Moreover, she reached out to colleagues for feedback on her ideas instead of isolating herself during this intense period.

As a result of these strategies, not only did Sarah meet her deadlines but she also emerged from the experience with greater confidence in her abilities—transforming what could have been a demoralizing challenge into an opportunity for growth.

Another example is Mark—a project lead who consistently met resistance from his team members during meetings due to differing priorities and communication styles. Rather than letting these conflicts chip away at his resolve, he took proactive steps by scheduling one-on-one sessions with each member.

During these conversations, he actively listened and sought input on their concerns while reinforcing shared goals for the project's success. Mark's approach transformed previously contentious interactions into collaborative problem-solving discussions, ultimately strengthening his team's cohesion and performance under pressure.

These narratives highlight how adopting strategies like mindfulness and building positive relationships can cultivate resilience in various contexts—empowering you to face workplace challenges confidently.

In summary, building mental resilience involves understanding its foundational role in professional success while implementing practical techniques that foster emotional intelligence and collaboration among colleagues. As you strengthen your mental fortitude through mindful practices and supportive relationships within your network, you'll find yourself better equipped not only to face adversity but also thrive amidst uncertainty—all while advancing along your career path.

* * *

Embracing Change as an Opportunity

Change is an inevitable part of any career. As professionals, we often find ourselves navigating shifts in company structures, job roles, or industry trends. Rather than resisting these changes, it's crucial to understand that embracing them can lead to personal and professional growth.

Recognizing and accepting change reduces anxiety and enhances adaptability. Think about it: when a project shifts direction or a new management team comes on board, those initial feelings of uncertainty can be overwhelming. Yet, acknowledging that change is a natural part of the work environment allows you to shift your perspective. It's not about whether the change will happen; it's about how you choose to respond to it.

When we open ourselves up to change, we often discover new doors of opportunity and innovation. A colleague might come up with fresh ideas during a restructuring process, or you might find that a new role allows you to explore uncharted territory in your skill set. This proactive approach toward change not only positions you as someone who can handle transitions with grace but also sets you apart as a leader in your organization.

CHAPTER 8: RESILIENCE AND ADAPTABILITY

To reframe change as positive requires intentional practice. Begin by identifying specific challenges that arise from upcoming changes in your workplace. Instead of viewing these challenges through a lens of negativity, ask yourself how they can serve as stepping stones for growth.

For instance, if you're facing a significant technology overhaul at work, instead of lamenting the loss of familiar tools and processes, consider how this transition could enhance your skills in cutting-edge software that might benefit your career long-term. Positive thinking significantly mitigates fears associated with change. It transforms worry into curiosity—what could I learn from this situation? What opportunities might emerge?

Cultivating an opportunity-focused mindset doesn't happen overnight; it requires consistent effort and reinforcement. Start small by incorporating affirmations into your daily routine that encourage resilience in the face of change. For example, repeat phrases like "I adapt easily to new situations" or "Every change brings new possibilities." These reminders can create a mental shift over time.

Examining examples of successful figures who have thrived amidst change offers relatable lessons and motivation. Consider the story of Howard Schultz, who transformed Starbucks from a small coffee shop into a global brand by embracing changes in consumer preferences and market trends. Schultz recognized early on that coffee culture was shifting toward quality over quantity and responded by introducing premium products and experiences.

By adapting to changing customer desires, Schultz didn't just save Starbucks; he revolutionized the coffee industry altogether. His journey underscores how embracing change can lead to groundbreaking outcomes—not just for individuals but for entire organizations.

These stories motivate us to adopt similar attitudes when faced with our own transitions. If others have navigated upheaval successfully, so can we—by maintaining flexibility and keeping an open mind. To navigate change effectively, there are several action steps readers can take right away:

1. **Set Personal Goals**: Define clear objectives for how you plan to adapt to new circumstances in your workplace. Perhaps you want to learn a new software program or engage more actively in team meetings during periods of transition.
2. **Seek Out Workshops and Resources**: Many organizations offer training programs specifically designed for handling workplace changes—take advantage of these resources! Engaging in continuous learning helps bolster your confidence when facing unfamiliar situations.
3. **Build a Dynamic Skill Set**: Developing versatile skills ensures you're well-prepared for whatever changes come your way—whether it's enhancing technical proficiencies or improving interpersonal communication abilities.

In summary, embracing change opens pathways for growth while fostering resilience within ourselves and our teams. By reframing our perspectives on transitions and actively seeking opportunities amid uncertainty, we not only elevate our own careers but contribute positively to the work environment around us.

* * *

Developing Flexibility in Work Approaches

In today's fast-paced professional landscape, flexibility is not just a desirable trait; it has become a crucial skill for thriving in diverse work environments. The ability to adapt your work style and strategies in response to changing circumstances can significantly enhance both individual performance and team dynamics.

Understanding what it means to be flexible in a professional context is the first step toward cultivating this essential skill. Flexibility goes hand in hand with resilience and adaptability. It enables you to overcome challenges that arise unexpectedly, whether it's shifting deadlines, changes in project scope, or evolving team dynamics. By remaining flexible, you can navigate these hurdles without losing sight of your overall goals.

Professionals who demonstrate flexibility often earn respect from their peers and superiors. Colleagues view them as reliable and resourceful, capable of handling the unpredictability that comes with modern work life. This respect can lead to greater collaboration opportunities and advancement within an organization.

To build flexibility into your daily work routine, consider implementing some practical strategies designed to enhance adaptability. Start by training yourself to adjust plans while maintaining focus on your goals. When an unforeseen issue arises—say a last-minute meeting that conflicts with a deadline—resist the urge to panic. Instead, take a moment to reassess your priorities and adjust your schedule accordingly. This kind of agility can help you maintain productivity while demonstrating your capacity for adaptability.

Creating contingency plans is another effective method for managing unexpected changes effectively. For instance, if you're working on a project with multiple stakeholders, anticipate potential roadblocks by identifying alternative paths forward should things not go as planned.

This foresight not only reduces stress when challenges arise but also prepares you to respond proactively rather than reactively.

Encouraging open-mindedness is vital in supporting the sensitive handling of varying work dynamics. A rigid mindset can stifle creativity and hinder collaboration among team members who may have different perspectives or approaches. By fostering an environment where diverse ideas are welcomed, you enhance both individual and collective problem-solving abilities.

To illustrate the impact of flexibility in action, consider organizations that thrive on flexible approaches. Many companies have embraced agile methodologies that prioritize adaptability over strict adherence to predefined plans. These organizations often see significant boosts in overall productivity and morale as teams collaborate more effectively amidst change.

Take Google, for example. The tech giant encourages its employees to allocate time for innovative projects outside their core responsibilities—a practice known as "20% time." This flexibility fosters a culture of innovation and creativity where employees feel empowered to explore new ideas without the constraints of traditional structures.

Furthermore, companies like Netflix have adapted quickly to external pressures by embracing flexible work models that prioritize results over rigid schedules or locations. Employees are trusted to manage their own time while focusing on delivering high-quality outcomes rather than merely clocking hours at their desks.

Evaluating your own flexibility within the workplace is equally important for personal growth. Start with self-reflection; identify any barriers that might be inhibiting your ability to adapt effectively. Are there specific situations where you find it challenging to shift gears? Acknowledging these moments will allow you to devise strategies for overcoming them in the future.

Constructive feedback loops from colleagues can enhance one's adaptability as well. Don't hesitate to seek input about how others perceive your response to change or unexpected developments at work. Feedback can provide valuable insights into areas where you might need improvement while also affirming your strengths.

Lastly, regularly practice scenarios where flexibility is required so you're better prepared for real-life applications when they arise. Role-playing potential workplace situations—like managing conflicting priorities or collaborating with different personalities—can build confidence in your ability to navigate change seamlessly when it occurs.

By actively cultivating flexibility within yourself and your team, you'll not only foster resilience but also create an environment conducive to growth and success amidst challenges inherent in modern work life.

* * *

Setting Boundaries to Avoid Burnout

Burnout has become a common buzzword in the professional world, but what does it really mean? Understanding burnout is crucial for anyone striving to maintain their energy and passion for work. It isn't just about feeling tired; it encompasses a range of emotional, physical, and mental exhaustion that results from prolonged stress. When you hit this wall, your productivity plummets, your creativity stagnates, and the enthusiasm you once had for your job dissipates.

Recognizing the early signs of stress is essential for proactive management. These signs can manifest in various ways: chronic fatigue, irritability, decreased performance, or a feeling of hopelessness. If you find yourself dreading Mondays or struggling to muster enthusiasm for projects you once enjoyed, it might be time to take a closer look at your work-life balance. Burnout often stems from poor boundaries—when work seeps into every corner of your life and leaves little room for personal time or relaxation.

Understanding that burnout isn't just an individual problem but often linked to workplace culture is vital. Many organizations inadvertently foster environments where employees feel they must constantly push beyond their limits. This awareness can lead to healthier coping mechanisms, enabling individuals to recognize when they need to step back and reassess their commitments.

So how do you establish boundaries that prevent burnout while enhancing productivity? Here are several techniques that can help:

1. Learn to Say No

One of the most powerful tools in setting boundaries is learning how to say no effectively. Many professionals struggle with this because they fear disappointing others or missing out on opportunities. However, taking on too much can lead to overwhelm and ultimately diminish your performance across the board.

When faced with additional requests, take a moment before responding. Ask yourself if saying yes aligns with your current priorities or if it will push you closer to burnout. You might say something like:

"I appreciate the offer; however, I have other commitments right now that I need to focus on."

This response is polite yet firm, allowing you to maintain control over your workload without sacrificing relationships.

2. Prioritize Your Tasks

Effective prioritization is another cornerstone of boundary-setting. Instead of tackling everything at once, create a hierarchy for your tasks based on urgency and importance. This approach not only clarifies what needs immediate attention but also helps avoid feelings of being overwhelmed by an endless list of responsibilities.

Consider using frameworks like the Eisenhower Matrix, which categorizes tasks into four quadrants: urgent and important, important but not urgent, urgent but not important, and neither urgent nor important. By focusing on what truly matters first, you can allocate your time and energy more efficiently while keeping burnout at bay.

3. Encourage Regular Breaks

Taking breaks might seem counterintuitive when trying to maximize productivity; however, regular pauses are essential for maintaining energy levels throughout the day. Whether it's a quick walk outside or a few minutes spent stretching at your desk, these short intermissions allow both your body and mind to recharge.

Make it a habit to schedule these breaks into your calendar as non-negotiable appointments with yourself. A simple reminder every hour can serve as an effective prompt—giving you permission to step away from work momentarily so that when you return, you're more focused and energized.

4. Prioritize Personal Time

Carving out personal time each week is crucial for recharging after busy workdays filled with meetings and deadlines. It's easy to neglect self-care when immersed in work demands; however, this neglect contributes significantly to feelings of burnout.

Set aside dedicated time for activities that nourish your spirit—whether it's reading a book by the bay window while sipping coffee or exploring hiking trails in the Rockies with family during weekends. Engaging in these pursuits not only enhances well-being but also fosters creativity that can spill over into your professional life.

Examples of Effective Boundary-Setting

The stories of professionals who have successfully managed their boundaries provide inspiration for anyone struggling with balance in their lives:

Take Sarah—a marketing manager who realized her workload was becoming unmanageable as she began staying late consistently just to keep up with demands from multiple clients. She decided enough was enough; she established clear office hours and communicated them firmly with her team members.

At first, there was pushback as colleagues were accustomed to asking her questions outside regular hours—yet over time they adjusted their expectations accordingly. The positive outcome? Not only did Sarah regain her evenings but her overall productivity increased during work hours as well since she was able to focus without constant interruptions after hours.

Another example involves James—a software development team leader who found himself increasingly stressed due to unrealistic project timelines imposed by his supervisor. After reflecting on his own limitations—and realizing he wasn't alone in feeling this pressure—he approached his boss with data illustrating how additional resources could improve project outcomes without leading employees toward burnout.

His supervisor listened attentively; together they devised more realistic timelines while advocating for support through team collaboration instead of solo pressure-cooking sessions filled with late-night coding marathons!

Both Sarah's and James' experiences emphasize how boundary-setting doesn't just benefit individuals—it cultivates an environment where everyone thrives collectively!

Tools for Continuous Boundary Assessment

As circumstances change—whether due to evolving workplace dynamics or personal commitments—it's essential not only initially set boundaries but also regularly assess them as well:

Consider implementing frameworks designed specifically for evaluating personal boundaries across various scenarios within professional contexts! Reflective practices such as journaling provide insight into whether certain areas require adjustments based on feedback received from colleagues about workload expectations vs capacity levels moving forward over time!

Engage in discussions around setting healthy boundaries within teams regularly—utilize group meetings focused solely on sharing insights regarding workload distribution among peers rather than merely task updates! These dialogues create opportunities not only strengthen relationships amongst coworkers but encourage collective accountability toward maintaining healthy limits!

In summary:

1. Recognize signs associated with burnout stemming from lack thereof;
2. Implement practical strategies around saying no + prioritizing effectively;
3. Schedule regular breaks alongside personal time weekly;

4. Learn from successful anecdotes showcasing how establishing clear limits yields satisfaction throughout one's career journey!

By embracing these approaches—alongside continual assessments—you'll cultivate an empowered atmosphere where individuals flourish collectively while sidestepping debilitating exhaustion commonly faced across many industries today!

Chapter 9: Cultivating a Growth Mindset

When I first heard the term "growth mindset," it struck a chord deep within me. This concept, popularized by psychologist Carol Dweck, represents an essential shift in how we perceive our abilities and potential. Rather than seeing intelligence and talent as fixed traits, a growth mindset encourages us to view them as qualities that can be developed through dedication and hard work. It's an empowering perspective that opens the door to learning and continuous improvement.

In this chapter, we'll explore several key topics designed to help you foster this growth-oriented mindset. First, we'll dive into the distinction between a fixed mindset and a growth mindset, illustrating how each approach shapes our reactions to challenges. Next, we'll discuss the importance of seeking feedback for improvement—how embracing constructive criticism can propel our development. Lifelong learning is another critical aspect we'll cover; after all, in today's fast-paced world, staying curious is vital for success. Lastly, we'll address the value of setting new challenges that stretch our limits and foster growth.

Together, these concepts will equip you with tools to cultivate resilience and adaptability in your professional journey.

* * *

Understanding Fixed vs. Growth Mindset

When we think about our capabilities, we often fall into one of two mindsets: a fixed mindset or a growth mindset. Understanding these concepts is crucial for anyone looking to enhance their confidence and promote success in their professional journey.

A **fixed mindset** believes that our abilities and intelligence are static traits—something we're born with and can't significantly change. Picture someone who thinks, "I'm just not good at public speaking," or "I'll never be able to learn this new software." This belief system can become a major roadblock. When faced with challenges, individuals with a fixed mindset may shy away from opportunities, fearing failure and avoiding risks altogether.

Recognizing traits associated with a fixed mindset is the first step toward change. You might notice tendencies like avoiding difficult tasks or feeling threatened by the success of others. Embracing challenges becomes daunting under this perspective; instead of seeing obstacles as chances to grow, they view them as threats to their self-worth.

On the other hand, a **growth mindset** fosters the belief that we can develop our skills through dedication and hard work. It's rooted in the idea that intelligence and talent are just starting points; what truly matters is our willingness to learn and adapt. Individuals who embrace this mindset welcome challenges rather than retreating from them. They understand that effort leads to improvement, which in turn boosts confidence.

A growth mindset encourages resilience in the face of challenges. When setbacks occur, those with this perspective see them as opportunities for learning rather than evidence of inadequacy. This attitude promotes a love for learning that contributes to greater career satisfaction over time.

CHAPTER 9: CULTIVATING A GROWTH MINDSET

Moreover, acknowledging effort as a determinant of success strengthens self-esteem. When you believe your hard work can lead to improvement, you start taking on new projects with enthusiasm rather than trepidation. This shift opens doors not only for personal development but also for professional growth.

The benefits of adopting a growth mindset extend beyond individual confidence—it influences workplace dynamics as well. People with a growth mindset are more likely to embrace feedback for improvement. Instead of viewing constructive criticism as personal attacks, they see it as valuable insights that can guide their development.

Additionally, individuals equipped with a growth mindset are better prepared to handle workplace adversities. They adapt more easily to changing circumstances because they see every challenge as an opportunity for further growth and skill enhancement.

Furthermore, a growth mindset fosters adaptive learning strategies. Those who adopt this approach seek out resources, ask questions, and engage in discussions that expand their understanding and capabilities. They cultivate curiosity about their field, which not only keeps them informed but also makes them more innovative contributors within their organizations.

Now that we've explored the definitions and benefits of fixed versus growth mindsets, how can you cultivate this transformative perspective in your own life? Here are some practical steps:

1. **Set Incremental Challenges**: Start small by setting manageable goals that push you just beyond your comfort zone. These incremental challenges promote constant skill improvement without overwhelming you.
2. **Regularly Reflect on Experiences**: Take time at the end of each day or week to reflect on what you've learned from your experiences—both successes and failures alike. This practice

enhances your adaptability and encourages ongoing learning.
3. **Engage with Mentors**: Find mentors who embody a growth mindset themselves. Their guidance can provide invaluable insights on shifting perspectives while also encouraging you to embrace new challenges without fear.

By understanding these concepts and implementing these strategies into your life, you'll begin cultivating a growth-oriented approach that enhances your confidence and propels you forward in your career journey.

***

Seeking Feedback for Improvement

Feedback stands as one of the most powerful tools for growth in both personal and professional realms. Embracing feedback allows us to learn, adapt, and enhance our skills. In a world that thrives on collaboration and innovation, understanding how to seek and utilize feedback effectively can create a robust framework for continuous improvement.

Value of Constructive Feedback

Constructive feedback holds immense value. It serves as a roadmap, offering clear insights into areas that require enhancement. When someone points out where I can improve—whether it's a presentation style, communication skills, or project management techniques—I gain an opportunity to refine my abilities. Instead of viewing such criticism as a personal affront, I learned to accept it as an essential part of my development journey.

This process transforms challenges into growth opportunities. For example, if I receive feedback on a project proposal's clarity, it highlights the specific elements needing revision. Acknowledging this enables me to address weaknesses proactively rather than defensively. Such dialogues encourage ongoing conversations about performance and progress, fostering an environment where everyone feels comfortable discussing strengths and weaknesses openly.

How to Ask for Feedback

Knowing how to ask for feedback is just as critical as receiving it. To get the most out of this process, clarify specific areas where you seek improvement. Rather than simply asking for general feedback—"How did I do?"—try framing your request with more precision: "Could you help me understand how I can improve my presentation delivery?" This approach focuses the conversation on particular aspects of your performance.

Timing and context also matter when seeking feedback. Consider requesting insights immediately after completing a task or presentation while the details are still fresh in others' minds. Setting aside time during team meetings dedicated solely to feedback encourages an atmosphere conducive to open dialogue about everyone's performance.

Moreover, creating a culture of openness can significantly enhance receptiveness among team members. Encourage your colleagues to share their thoughts candidly by modeling this behavior yourself—showing appreciation for constructive criticism when you receive it can lead others to feel comfortable doing the same.

Responding to Feedback

Once you have received feedback, how you respond plays a crucial role in your development process. Taking time to reflect on the insights shared before reacting fosters thoughtful responses instead of knee-jerk reactions fueled by defensiveness or insecurity.

It's important to distinguish between factual feedback and personal opinions as well. Not all critiques are grounded in objective truth; some may stem from individual preferences or biases. Keeping this distinction in mind helps protect self-esteem while allowing you to glean valuable lessons from each piece of advice.

After processing the feedback, developing action plans based on what you've learned ensures continuous improvement. Break down specific steps that incorporate suggestions received into your daily routine or upcoming projects; this method keeps you accountable while actively demonstrating that you're committed to growth.

Leveraging Peer Feedback

The benefits of seeking peer feedback cannot be overstated—it fosters collaboration and teamwork within any organization. By encouraging mutual exchanges of insights among colleagues, we create an atmosphere rich with diverse perspectives that enrich our understanding.

Establishing regular check-ins with team members invites ongoing discussions about individual performances and goals over time rather than limiting these conversations to annual reviews or specific project completions. These informal gatherings cultivate camaraderie while making constructive criticism commonplace rather than feared.

Asking peers for their input offers numerous advantages; often they notice patterns we might overlook due to familiarity with our work styles or approaches. Encouraging input from those outside our immediate responsibilities broadens our perspectives even further and invites new ideas that could revolutionize our projects or practices altogether.

Feedback shouldn't be viewed solely through the lens of criticism; it's an invaluable opportunity for learning—and one that paves the way toward achieving higher levels of confidence and competence throughout our careers.

In navigating professional landscapes marked by constant change and competition, honing the ability to seek out—and graciously receive—feedback sets individuals apart as they foster growth-oriented career trajectories capable of overcoming obstacles effectively.

* * *

Embracing Lifelong Learning

Lifelong learning refers to the ongoing, voluntary, and self-motivated pursuit of knowledge for personal or professional development. In a professional context, it embodies a commitment to continuous improvement, adaptation, and growth in response to ever-evolving work environments. This learning can take many forms—formal education, self-study through books and online resources, or experiential learning gained from hands-on experiences in the workplace.

As workplaces rapidly evolve due to technological advancements and shifting market demands, embracing lifelong learning becomes essential. Organizations increasingly value employees who demonstrate adaptability and a proactive approach to skill enhancement. In essence, a commitment to lifelong learning not only enhances employability prospects but also positions individuals as invaluable assets within their teams.

Benefits of Lifelong Learning

The advantages of adopting a lifelong learning mindset extend far beyond simply acquiring new knowledge. Continuous learning fuels innovation and creativity in the workplace. When employees engage in ongoing education—whether through workshops, seminars, or online courses—they cultivate fresh ideas and approaches that can lead to improved processes and innovative solutions. This not only benefits the individual but can also propel entire teams or organizations forward.

Moreover, lifelong learning enhances resilience against industry changes and job displacement. In an era where job roles can shift dramatically within a short period, those who actively seek new skills are better prepared to pivot when necessary. By staying ahead of trends and expanding their skill sets, they reduce the risk of becoming obsolete in their fields.

Beyond practical implications for career stability, lifelong learning instills confidence in taking on new roles and responsibilities. As individuals broaden their expertise through continuous education, they build a foundation of knowledge that allows them to tackle unfamiliar tasks with greater assurance. This newfound confidence often translates into higher performance levels and greater satisfaction at work.

Practical Ways to Engage in Lifelong Learning

Integrating lifelong learning into your daily routine doesn't have to be daunting; there are several practical strategies you can employ to make it a habit. One effective method is setting personal development goals related to skill enhancement. By defining specific areas where you want to grow—be it mastering a software tool relevant to your field or improving your public speaking abilities—you create a roadmap for your educational journey.

Attending workshops, seminars, and online courses is another way to keep your knowledge fresh while engaging with industry experts and like-minded peers. Many organizations offer professional development opportunities that align with current market demands; taking advantage of these resources not only broadens your skills but also expands your network within the industry.

Networking with other learners fosters shared experiences that enhance the overall educational process. Joining professional associations or study groups creates an environment conducive to collaborative learning; exchanging insights with others often leads to deeper understanding and fresh perspectives on various topics.

Creating a Learning Mindset

To truly embrace lifelong learning, cultivating a mindset focused on ongoing education is crucial. Celebrating small wins in your learning journey boosts motivation and enthusiasm for continued growth. Each time you complete an online course or apply newly acquired skills successfully at work, take a moment to acknowledge this achievement—no matter how minor it may seem.

Encouraging curiosity by asking questions stimulates exploration both personally and professionally. Approach challenges with an inquisitive mindset: What can I learn from this situation? How might different perspectives change my understanding? Such inquiries promote engagement with content rather than passive absorption of information.

Lastly, embracing failure as an opportunity for learning reduces the fear associated with risk-taking. Everyone encounters setbacks; viewing them as valuable lessons rather than personal shortcomings fosters resilience while encouraging experimentation in various contexts. When you understand that mistakes are part of the process rather than endpoints on your path toward mastery, you position yourself for continued success over time.

By committing yourself wholeheartedly to lifelong learning—and implementing these strategies—you lay the groundwork for an enriching career characterized by adaptability and sustained growth amidst ever-changing landscapes.

* * *

Setting New Challenges for Growth

When it comes to personal development, setting new challenges plays a pivotal role. Challenges act as catalysts that propel us out of our comfort zones and into spaces where growth flourishes. If you want to expand your horizons, embracing the discomfort of challenge is essential.

Stepping outside of what feels familiar can feel intimidating, but it accelerates personal development in ways you might not expect. Each time I faced a challenge, I discovered untapped potential within myself. I realized I could tackle tasks that once seemed daunting, uncovering strengths I had never acknowledged. Every obstacle I overcame reinforced my self-efficacy—the belief in my ability to succeed—ultimately boosting my confidence.

So how do you go about identifying the right challenges? It begins with an honest assessment of your current skill levels. What are you good at? Where do you excel? Pinpointing your strengths is crucial for selecting appropriate challenges that won't overwhelm you but rather inspire growth. For instance, if you're comfortable presenting ideas in

CHAPTER 9: CULTIVATING A GROWTH MINDSET

small groups, consider taking on the challenge of speaking at a larger event or workshop.

Aim for challenges that stretch your capabilities without breaking them. The goal is not to drown in stress but to find an edge where learning occurs. Perhaps this means volunteering for a leadership role on a project or committing to lead training sessions within your organization. Each challenge should align with both your personal interests and professional goals, ensuring that it contributes positively to your growth trajectory.

Long-term goals serve as a compass when choosing challenges. By considering where you want to be in five or ten years, you can identify relevant obstacles that will move you forward. If you aspire to climb the corporate ladder, think about skills or experiences that would make you more qualified for those roles. Seek challenges that prepare you for future opportunities while also nurturing immediate growth.

Once you've set these new challenges, it's essential to develop mechanisms for tracking your progress along the way. A learning journal or blog, even private, can become a valuable tool for documenting experiences and reflections related to each challenge faced. Writing down not just what you've accomplished but also how you've felt throughout the process creates a rich narrative of growth over time.

Establishing milestone markers is another effective strategy for motivation during challenging periods. By breaking down larger challenges into smaller tasks and celebrating their completion, you can maintain momentum while reinforcing feelings of achievement along the way.

Accountability partners also enhance commitment levels when pursuing new challenges. Find someone who shares similar goals or interests and commit together to tackle obstacles head-on. This partnership fosters encouragement and accountability, making it less likely for either person to give up when faced with difficulties.

Recognizing achievements is just as crucial as setting challenges in the first place. Reflecting on milestones reached through these endeavors reinforces a sense of accomplishment and growth—an acknowledgment that each step taken contributes significantly toward larger aspirations.

Take time after completing each challenge to celebrate your achievements consciously; whether through a simple acknowledgment or by treating yourself to something special, it matters! These moments of reflection allow deeper learning experiences and provide clarity on what worked well—and what didn't—during the journey.

Moreover, sharing successes with peers creates community support around your achievements while inspiring others on similar paths toward growth and development. Engaging with colleagues about how you've tackled obstacles opens doors for collaborative conversations and motivates others to face their own set of challenges.

In summary, pursuing new challenges enhances self-confidence while facilitating personal development by encouraging us all to reach higher than we thought possible; these pursuits help illuminate our strengths while building resilience against setbacks encountered along the way!

Chapter 10: Empowering Future Leadership

As I progressed in my career, the idea of leadership evolved from a distant aspiration to a tangible goal. I recognized that true leadership extends beyond authority or title; it requires the ability to inspire and uplift others while fostering an inclusive environment. Preparing for leadership roles with confidence means embracing not just personal growth but also a commitment to cultivating a culture where everyone feels valued and empowered.

In this chapter, I will delve into several essential topics that will guide you on your journey toward becoming an influential leader.

First, we'll explore ***developing leadership skills***. Building a robust skill set is crucial for effective leadership. It involves honing abilities like communication, decision-making, and emotional intelligence—skills that not only enhance your own capabilities but also enable you to guide others with clarity and purpose. I'll share insights from my own experiences and the practical steps I've taken to cultivate these vital skills.

Next, we'll discuss ***influencing with integrity***. Leadership without integrity falls flat; it breeds mistrust and disengagement. Integrity builds the foundation for authentic connections with your team. I learned early on that leading with honesty and transparency fosters an environment where people feel safe to voice their ideas and concerns.

In this section, I'll highlight strategies for embodying integrity in your leadership style.

We can't overlook the importance of **promoting diversity and inclusion** in our workplaces. A diverse team brings a wealth of perspectives that enriches problem-solving and innovation. Throughout my career, I witnessed firsthand how diverse teams outperform homogeneous ones—not just in creativity but also in employee satisfaction and retention rates. Here, we'll examine actionable ways to champion diversity within your organization, ensuring everyone has a seat at the table.

Finally, we'll dive into **vision setting for personal and organizational growth**. Every effective leader needs a clear vision—one that aligns with both personal values and organizational goals. This vision serves as a roadmap that guides decision-making while inspiring others to rally behind shared objectives. I'll share how I articulated my vision early in my journey and how it shaped my path forward.

As we embark on this exploration of empowering future leadership, remember: the leaders of tomorrow will shape workplaces into environments where everyone thrives together. Each topic will equip you with knowledge and practical strategies necessary to lead confidently while fostering inclusivity within your team.

* * *

Developing Leadership Skills

Effective leadership requires a unique blend of skills and qualities. As aspiring leaders, it's crucial to cultivate essential competencies that not only foster confidence but also enhance capability. Understanding these core competencies forms the bedrock of successful leadership.

CHAPTER 10: EMPOWERING FUTURE LEADERSHIP

Understanding Core Competencies

To navigate the complexities of modern workplaces, leaders must possess both soft and hard skills. Soft skills, such as communication, empathy, and conflict resolution, are vital for fostering relationships and maintaining team morale. These skills help leaders connect with their teams on a personal level, creating an environment where everyone feels valued and heard.

On the other hand, hard skills like strategic planning, project management, and data analysis enable leaders to make informed decisions. Balancing these two categories of skills allows leaders to adapt to various situations effectively.

Adaptability stands out as a critical attribute in leadership. In an ever-changing work environment, being flexible enough to adjust strategies in response to new challenges is essential. Alongside adaptability, emotional intelligence plays a pivotal role in understanding team dynamics and responding to the emotional needs of colleagues. Recognizing the significance of these competencies lays the foundation for continuous skill development, which promotes both confidence and credibility.

Practical Leadership Training

Once you identify the necessary competencies, the next step is acquiring them through practical training. Various training programs can aid in developing these leadership capabilities.

Mentorship and coaching are two vital tools that can significantly impact your growth as a leader. A mentor can provide insights based on their experiences while guiding you through challenges they've faced in their own careers. Coaching focuses more on specific skills or goals—think of it as personalized guidance tailored to your individual needs.

Additionally, role-playing and simulations offer hands-on experience that prepares aspiring leaders for real-world situations. These exercises allow you to practice decision-making in controlled environments without fear of real-life consequences. By engaging in simulations that mimic challenging scenarios you may encounter at work, you gain invaluable insights into your decision-making processes and communication styles.

Feedback is another critical element in leadership development. Constructive criticism helps illuminate blind spots you may not recognize in yourself. Taking time to reflect on this feedback fosters a growth mindset—one that embraces learning from mistakes rather than shying away from them.

Implementing Leadership Programs

Creating or participating in structured leadership development initiatives within organizations ensures continuous learning opportunities for all employees aspiring to lead. These programs can take various forms: workshops, seminars, or even online courses focused on specific leadership topics.

Collaboration among teams is equally important when developing collective leadership skills. Encourage open dialogues about leadership experiences within your organization; sharing stories fosters community learning while enhancing trust among team members. Building collaborative networks reinforces individual efforts by creating an environment where everyone learns from each other's strengths and weaknesses.

Advocating for ongoing education as part of professional development is key for nurturing confident leaders who can tackle challenges head-on. Consider establishing formalized training sessions that emphasize different aspects of leadership—from managing conflict effectively to developing strategic visions.

Leadership Experience

While structured training is essential, real-world experience remains one of the best teachers when it comes to building confidence as a leader. Engaging in hands-on opportunities provides invaluable insights that theoretical learning often cannot replicate.

Proactively seeking involvement in projects or committees enhances your exposure to diverse situations requiring leadership intervention. Whether leading a team initiative or facilitating a workshop, these experiences help solidify your understanding of what effective leadership looks like in practice.

Analyzing case studies of successful leaders serves as another form of inspiration while highlighting valuable lessons learned throughout their journeys. Reflecting on how they navigated challenges can guide your own approach when faced with similar obstacles.

In conclusion, cultivating essential leadership skills involves recognizing core competencies required for effective guidance—emphasizing adaptability and emotional intelligence alongside traditional hard skills; leveraging mentorship opportunities; engaging with role-playing simulations; promoting structured educational programs; seeking hands-on experiences—all while drawing lessons from those who have come before us on this path toward empowered leadership.

* * *

Influencing with Integrity

Integrity serves as the backbone of effective leadership. When you lead with integrity, you not only inspire trust but also foster a sense of respect among your team members. The significance of ethical behavior in leadership cannot be overstated; it is the foundation upon which strong relationships are built.

The Role of Ethics in Leadership

Ethical behavior is paramount in any professional environment. When leaders demonstrate integrity, they set a standard that resonates throughout their teams. This commitment to ethical conduct cultivates an atmosphere where honesty and transparency reign supreme.

Honesty means being straightforward with your team about expectations, challenges, and outcomes. When team members know that they can rely on their leader to be forthright, they feel more secure in their roles. This sense of security translates into greater productivity and collaboration.

Consider this: when faced with a challenging decision, it's easy to take the path that may seem expedient or beneficial in the short term. However, leading with integrity demands that you prioritize ethical decision-making—even when it's difficult. The way you navigate these challenges speaks volumes about your character and influences how your team perceives you.

When ethical dilemmas arise, leaders must evaluate not just the immediate impact of their decisions but also the long-term consequences for both individuals and the organization as a whole. By advocating for ethical behavior even under pressure, leaders reinforce a culture of trust and respect.

CHAPTER 10: EMPOWERING FUTURE LEADERSHIP

Building Trust within Teams

To cultivate an environment rooted in trust, open communication must be at the forefront. Encouraging team members to express their thoughts freely fosters an atmosphere where ideas can flourish without fear of ridicule or dismissal.

Shared values play an equally critical role in establishing a trusting environment. When teams have common goals and values, members are more likely to collaborate effectively toward achieving those objectives. It's essential for leaders to articulate these shared values clearly and consistently so everyone is aligned.

Consistency between actions and words is crucial for establishing credibility. If you say one thing but do another, you risk eroding trust among your team members. They need to see that you follow through on commitments; doing so reinforces their confidence in your leadership.

Creating feedback loops further enhances trust within teams. Regular check-ins where team members can provide insights or voice concerns allow everyone to feel heard and valued. This process not only improves communication but also strengthens relationships by fostering openness.

Empowering Others through Influence

Leaders wield significant influence over their teams—an influence that can be positive when exercised ethically. To empower others while maintaining integrity involves encouraging collaboration among diverse perspectives.

By valuing different viewpoints, leaders can create an inclusive environment where everyone feels appreciated for their contributions. This approach boosts morale and motivates individuals to put forth their best efforts because they know their input matters.

The principles of servant leadership align perfectly with this ethos of empowerment. Servant leaders prioritize the needs of their team members above all else, helping them develop professionally while enhancing overall team cohesion. When individuals feel supported by their leader's guidance, they become more engaged and motivated to excel.

Recognition and appreciation play vital roles in cultivating loyalty among team members as well. Taking time to acknowledge hard work—whether through verbal praise or formal awards—shows employees that their efforts do not go unnoticed. This acknowledgment reinforces commitment to both personal success and organizational goals.

Navigating Ethical Dilemmas

Even with a strong foundation built on integrity, ethical dilemmas will inevitably arise during your leadership journey. Navigating these situations requires careful consideration through an ethical lens—a skill all effective leaders should cultivate.

When faced with tough choices, utilizing frameworks can aid in analyzing options objectively while considering potential ramifications on all stakeholders involved. These frameworks serve as guides that encourage thoughtful reflection rather than hasty decisions based solely on immediate outcomes.

Real-life examples abound illustrating how leaders successfully navigated ethical challenges while upholding integrity under pressure. Whether it's addressing conflicts of interest or managing sensitive information, history offers lessons from those who chose ethics over convenience—even when it cost them personally or professionally.

Encouraging your team to speak up about ethical concerns empowers them further while fostering transparency within your organization culture as a whole—a culture where moral courage is rewarded rather than penalized creates resilience against unethical practices down the line.

As you navigate these complex waters as a leader committed to influencing others with integrity...

* * *

Promoting Diversity and Inclusion

Fostering a diverse and inclusive workplace is not just a moral imperative; it's essential for enhancing leadership effectiveness and creating a supportive environment for everyone involved. When organizations prioritize diversity, they unlock a wealth of perspectives that drive innovation and creativity.

Diverse teams generate richer problem-solving capabilities because they bring different viewpoints to the table. Each member contributes unique experiences and ideas, leading to more robust decision-making processes. A company that embraces diversity not only improves its internal dynamics but also enhances its reputation in the marketplace. Clients and customers increasingly prefer to engage with organizations that reflect their values, which includes a commitment to diversity. In turn, this commitment attracts top talent from various backgrounds who are eager to join an inclusive environment.

Moreover, a diverse leadership team can provide a significant competitive edge. Such leaders are better equipped to understand and connect with an equally varied customer base. Their experiences allow them to make decisions that resonate more deeply with diverse clientele, ultimately leading to better business outcomes.

To implement inclusive practices effectively, organizations must take actionable steps toward promoting inclusivity in every aspect of their operations. Bias training is crucial in this effort; raising awareness around unconscious biases helps reduce discrimination at all levels. Companies should actively create equitable opportunities for all employees by ensuring fair recruitment processes and advancement pathways.

Open dialogue about diversity issues should be encouraged throughout the organization. Creating safe spaces where employees feel comfortable discussing these topics fosters an inclusive culture where everyone's voice matters.

Championing diversity within leadership is vital as well. Representation matters—not only does it inspire those from underrepresented backgrounds to pursue leadership roles, but it also reinforces the notion that diverse perspectives are valued at the highest levels of decision-making. Mentorship programs can play a key role in supporting these individuals on their journey toward leadership positions.

Additionally, organizations should advocate for policies that support diverse hiring practices, actively seeking candidates from various backgrounds during recruitment drives.

To ensure that these initiatives are effective, companies must measure their inclusivity success through specific metrics and reporting mechanisms tailored to track diversity progress over time. Regular reviews and adaptations of diversity policies will keep the focus sharp on inclusivity goals, fostering accountability at all levels of leadership for these critical objectives.

By understanding the value of diversity and implementing strategic initiatives, organizations can create environments where everyone feels supported and empowered to contribute their best work.

* * *

CHAPTER 10: EMPOWERING FUTURE LEADERSHIP

Vision Setting for Personal and Organizational Growth

Crafting a compelling vision serves as the cornerstone for both personal development and organizational success. A clear and inspiring vision not only fuels motivation but also provides a sense of direction that can steer individuals and teams through challenges.

When I think about what makes a vision statement powerful, several key elements come to mind. First, it needs to resonate deeply with its stakeholders—those who will live out that vision day in and day out. A strong vision is succinct, memorable, and reflects the core values of the organization or individual. It paints a picture of the desired future that excites and inspires people to contribute toward that goal.

Take a moment to consider what values are central to you or your organization. How do these values inform your vision? Aligning personal and organizational values creates a unified purpose, enabling everyone involved to pull in the same direction. This alignment fosters a collective sense of ownership over the vision, making it more likely for individuals to invest their time and energy into realizing it.

Looking at successful leaders can provide valuable lessons in this regard. For example, consider Howard Schultz of Starbucks. His vision for Starbucks extended beyond merely selling coffee; he envisioned creating a "third place" between home and work where people could connect over coffee. Schultz communicated this vision consistently, weaving it into every aspect of Starbucks' culture—from employee training to customer experience—making it clear that this was more than just a business; it was about community.

Once you have crafted a compelling vision, the next crucial step is communicating that vision effectively. Clarity and enthusiasm are vital here; without them, even the best-laid plans may fall flat. One powerful technique I've found particularly effective is storytelling. A well-told story can evoke emotions and create connections among team members, drawing them closer to the vision. When you share stories—whether they're anecdotes from your own experiences or narratives from others who have embraced similar visions—you bring life to abstract ideas.

Repetition also plays an essential role in ensuring your message resonates with others. Sharing your vision consistently helps embed it into the culture of your organization or within your own mindset. This doesn't mean parroting the same phrases over and over; rather, it involves finding fresh ways to express core ideas so they continue to engage your audience.

Inclusive discussions around the vision are equally important. Engaging others in dialogue allows diverse insights to emerge, fostering buy-in from various perspectives within the team or organization. Encourage feedback on how the vision aligns with their experiences or aspirations—it enriches understanding and deepens commitment.

After establishing your compelling vision and ensuring everyone is aligned with it, it's time to set strategic goals that translate that vision into actionable steps. This is where frameworks like SMART goals come into play—Specific, Measurable, Achievable, Relevant, Time-bound goals break down lofty ambitions into manageable tasks.

For instance, if your vision aims for increased innovation within your organization, one SMART goal might be: "By Q3 2024, implement three new product ideas generated through cross-departmental brainstorming sessions." This clarity enables teams to focus on concrete actions rather than abstract concepts.

Alignment between individual team objectives and overarching organizational goals is critical here too. Each member should understand how their specific contributions fit within the larger framework of the organization's aspirations—this clarity breeds accountability while reinforcing collective purpose.

CHAPTER 10: EMPOWERING FUTURE LEADERSHIP

Flexibility in goal setting remains vital as well; circumstances often shift unexpectedly in today's fast-paced environment. While having clear targets provides structure, adapting those targets when necessary ensures continued relevance in pursuit of the vision.

As you work toward realizing your vision through strategic goals, regular evaluation becomes essential for assessing progress along the way. Performance reviews can provide critical insights into what's working well—and what isn't—allowing for informed adjustments when necessary.

Celebrating milestones during this journey cannot be overstated either! Recognition boosts morale while reinforcing progress toward achieving long-term objectives; taking time to acknowledge small wins fuels ongoing motivation across teams.

Finally—and perhaps most importantly—embracing adaptive strategies ensures resilience when obstacles arise during implementation efforts. Challenges are inevitable in any endeavor aimed at growth; however, having proactive plans allows organizations (and individuals) not only to respond effectively but also to learn from setbacks as part of their evolution toward fulfilling their shared aspirations.

By setting a compelling vision grounded in core values while effectively communicating its essence throughout all levels of engagement—with clear action plans established via SMART goal-setting methods—we lay solid foundations for sustained personal growth alongside broader organizational success.

Conclusion

As we reach the end of our exploration together, I invite you to pause and reflect on the journey we've shared within these pages. This book was not just a collection of strategies and insights; it was a heartfelt invitation to rediscover your innate potential, cultivate unshakable confidence, and navigate the complexities of the professional landscape with grace and resilience.

Throughout this journey, we have delved into the essence of what it means to be confidently you, explored the hurdles that often obstruct our path, and uncovered the profound impact of self-belief on every aspect of your life. By taking the time to invest in yourself, you've made a powerful choice—a choice that sets the stage for growth, empowerment, and extraordinary achievements.

The Importance of Your Journey

Your journey of developing workplace confidence is not an isolated experience; it is a shared human experience that connects us all. We've touched on key elements such as understanding the roots of self-doubt and navigating the throes of impostor syndrome—a condition that many battle, yet few acknowledge. By bringing these issues to light, we have created an environment where it's safe to explore the multifaceted nature of confidence.

You've embarked on a path that equips you to face challenges with a renewed sense of purpose. You've learned the importance of embracing your unique strengths, harnessing your potential, and recognizing the value you contribute to your organization and community. Each lesson woven through the chapters of this book serves as a stepping stone towards liberating yourself from the constraints of fear and hesitation.

A Heartfelt Thank You

Thank you for dedicating your time, energy, and heart to embrace the teachings shared within this book. Growth is no small task, and the commitment you've demonstrated speaks volumes about your readiness to break through barriers and reach new heights. As you immerse yourself in your newfound confidence, remember that this transformation does not happen overnight. It requires ongoing practice, reflection, and the willingness to step outside of your comfort zone.

Celebrate every step—every realization and every moment of bravery. These incremental victories form the essence of your journey. Just as you wouldn't expect to become a master chef after cooking one meal, don't expect your confidence to flourish without nurturing it. Some days will be challenging, and self-doubt may rear its head again, but those moments serve as beautiful reminders of your resilience and courage.

Your Future is Bright

As you look to the future, keep in mind that confidence is a lifelong pursuit. With the tools and strategies you now have in your arsenal, seize opportunities to develop your skills further. The world is brimming with possibilities waiting for you to explore! Embrace learning opportunities, stay curious, and continue to push your boundaries.

Remember that the energy you cultivate within yourself ripples out into your environment. As you radiate confidence, you inspire those around you to do the same. Your voice matters, and your contributions have the power to spark change. Imagine the ripple effect you'll create as you step into your true potential—encouraging your colleagues to share their insights, motivating them to take risks, and uplifting those who may feel overshadowed by doubt.

A Gentle Reminder

If you've found value in this book, reconnecting through reviews, discussions, or recommendations is one incredible way to share the messages of empowerment and growth with others. A few moments of your time could light the way for someone else seeking the same transformative journey you have embarked upon.

Your voice can be instrumental in spreading this knowledge, encouraging others to unlock their confidence. Together, we can foster communities that uplift and empower, creating a world where everyone feels valued and capable of claiming their place. Please leave a review on Amazon with this this QR code:

CONCLUSION

Next Steps on Your Journey

As you close this book, keep in mind that you hold the key to your growth and success. Your potential is limitless. Keep striving toward your goals, keep learning, and importantly, keep believing in yourself. This journey is uniquely yours, filled with personal experiences, challenges, and triumphs that will shape every step you take.

So go out there with confidence! Share your ideas, speak up in meetings, and forge connections with authentic energy. Know that you are equipped to tackle whatever comes your way. The world needs your unique talents, your insights, and your leadership.

Thank you for allowing me to be part of your journey. Here's to a future filled with confidence, courage, and endless accomplishments. Your journey continues, and with it, the boundless opportunities that await you. Embrace them wholeheartedly—you've got this!

Resources

10 Proven Strategies for Mastering time management and Boosting Productivity. (n.d.). https://www.centraltest.com/blog/mastering-time-management-proven-strategies-balance-priorities-and-productivity

All about imposter syndrome. (n.d.). New Year Improved You Cultivating a Healthy Mind and Body. https://grad.uc.edu/student-life/news/all-about-imposter-syndrome.html

Bissel, E. (n.d.). *The power of allyship in the workplace: building inclusive and supportive work cultures.* https://www.inclusivv.co/blog/the-power-of-allyship-in-the-workplace-building-inclusive-and-supportive-work-cultures

British Heart Foundation. (n.d.). Active listening. *British Heart Foundation.* https://www.bhf.org.uk/informationsupport/heart-matters-magazine/wellbeing/how-to-talk-about-health-problems/active-listening

Clinic, C. (2024, October 24). *7 ways to improve your active listening skills.* Cleveland Clinic. https://health.clevelandclinic.org/active-listening

Cuncic, A., MA. (2024, September 23). *Is impostor syndrome holding you back from living your best life?* Verywell Mind. https://www.verywellmind.com/imposter-syndrome-and-social-anxiety-disorder-4156469

CWU Learning Commons. (n.d.). *GROWTH VS. FIXED MINDSET.* https://www.cwu.edu/academics/academic-resources/learning-commons/_documents/cwu-growth-vs-fixed-mindset-lc.pdf

RESOURCES

Drury University. (2022, August 8). Ten Reasons Why Diversity in Leadership is Crucial. *Drury University.* https://www.drury.edu/business/ten-reasons-why-diversity-in-leadership-is-crucial/

Goland, J. (2023, October 6). *Growth Mindset and Why it's Important in the Workplace | InVista Insights.* InVista Insights. https://invistainsights.com/blogs/growth-mindset-and-why-its-important-in-the-workplace/

How to network on social media like a pro. (2023, December 22). *BDC.ca.* https://www.bdc.ca/en/articles-tools/entrepreneurial-skills/improve-networking/5-tips-to-network-on-social-media-like-a-pro

Is Your Workplace Communication Style As Effective As It Could Be? - Professional & Executive Development | Harvard DCE. (2024, January 8). Professional & Executive Development | Harvard DCE. https://professional.dce.harvard.edu/blog/is-your-workplace-communication-style-as-effective-as-it-could-be/

Kw. (2014, May 19). *Microaggressions and being assertive.* Contemporary Racism. https://contemporaryracism.org/941/microaggressions-and-being-assertive/

Lcsw, S. M. D. (2022, September 16). Learning to set limits at work can protect you from job stress. *Psychology Today.* https://www.psychologytoday.com/us/blog/conquering-codependency/202209/how-better-boundaries-can-prevent-burnout

Lcsw, S. M. D. (2023, September 8). Accept that you're imperfect, and comfort yourself like a baby. *Psychology Today.* https://www.psychologytoday.com/us/blog/conquering-codependency/202306/8-simple-strategies-to-boost-self-compassion

Learn and Grow: What is adaptability in the workplace? | It's Your Yale. (n.d.). https://your.yale.edu/learn-and-grow-what-adaptability-workplace

Lparsons. (2024, January 8). *How to Build Business Relationships - Professional & Executive Development | Harvard DCE.* Professional &

Executive Development | Harvard DCE. https://professional.dce.harvard.edu/blog/how-to-build-business-relationships/

Marsh, E. (n.d.). *Personal development and the power of feedback.* https://www.t-three.com/thinking-space/blog/personal-development-and-the-power-of-feedback

Nonverbal Communication and its Impact in the Professional Environment. (n.d.). https://teambuilding.coddygames.com/en/blog/tips/nonverbal-communication-and-impact-team

Overcoming Self-Criticism | Counseling Services. (2017, November 7). https://counseling.uoregon.edu/overcoming-self-criticism

Paulise, L. (2022, September 16). *9 Signs that you have Impostor Syndrome.* Forbes. https://www.forbes.com/sites/lucianapaulise/2022/09/16/9-signs-that-you-have-impostor-syndrome/

Romero, J. (2024, December 27). *Managing Stress in High-Pressure work environments.* WorkCare. https://workcare.com/managing-stress-in-high-pressure-work-environments/

Rose, T. (2024, October 28). *9 Women in tech share their stories about imposter syndrome.* Built In. https://builtin.com/articles/9-women-tech-share-their-stories-about-imposter-syndrome

Sullivan, K. (2020, August 18). *MORE GOOD NEWS FOR LGBTQ COMMUNITY.* Barrett & Farahany. https://www.justiceatwork.com/5-ways-to-document-employment-discrimination/

Susanne. (2024, August 12). Celebrating Successes: how to boost self-esteem and motivation • Passionate Writer Coaching. *Passionate Writer Coaching.* https://passionatewritercoaching.com/celebrating-successes/

Printed in Great Britain
by Amazon